In Memory of Janet Hunter and Jenny Cooper, wives and mothers who lost their husbands and providers at the Somme in 1916. These two women fought their way through two world wars, not in the armed forces but on the Home Front. Like many other Scottish women, without the help of a National Health Service or Social Security system, they worked long hours in the cold and damp woollen mills to support their families. Janet and Jenny, my grandmother and great-aunt, struggled on till at age 60 they were rewarded with a gold watch and osteoarthritis.

History books preoccupied with the accomplishments of men, have forgotten the armies of heroines that held this country together. In neglecting to record women's lives, history has denied women not only knowledge of their mothers but knowledge of themselves.

Scotland's Hidden Harlots and Heroines

Women's role in Scottish society from 1690–1969

Annie Harrower-Gray

First published in Great Britain in 2014 by
Pen & Sword Social History
an imprint of
Pen & Sword Books Ltd
47 Church Street
Barnsley
South Yorkshire
S70 2AS

ISBN 978 1 78159 271 7

A CIP catalogue record for this book is available from the British Library

Typeset in Ehrhardt by
Mac Style, Bridlington, East Yorkshire
Printed and bound in the UK by CPI Group (UK) Ltd, Croydon, CRO 4YY

Pen & Sword Books Ltd incorporates the imprints of Pen & Sword Archaeology, Atlas, Aviation, Battleground, Discovery, Family History, History, Maritime, Military, Naval, Politics, Railways, Select, Transport, True Crime, and Fiction, Frontline Books, Leo Cooper, Praetorian Press, Seaforth Publishing and Wharncliffe.

For a complete list of Pen & Sword titles please contact
PEN & SWORD BOOKS LIMITED
47 Church Street, Barnsley, South Yorkshire, S70 2AS, England
E-mail: enquiries@pen-and-sword.co.uk
Website: www.pen-and-sword.co.uk

Contents

Acknowledgements

Scotland's Hidden Harlots and Heroines includes only a small part of the history of all the women who have helped make this great nation what it is today. I couldn't have told even this fraction of the story on my own, though. As always Pauline Campbell at Anstruther Library, found some of the most obscure books for me and kept me on the straight and narrow when my fines looked as if they might be getting out of hand. Paul Hambleton at the National Library of Scotland helped with the online stuff there, while Mark Boulay and Special Collections at University of St Andrews allowed me to use their wonderful photographs.

Thanks to Sharon Reid for her willingness to muck in and help me with research, as well as all at Pen and Sword, especially my editor Jen Newby, who has shown unwavering support and patience, and Dom Allen for his wonderful cover. I'm not sure if it's Lady Macbeth screaming through the glen or Colonel Anne MacKintosh looking for a place to hide Bonnie Prince Charlie, but the wifies having their tea don't seem bothered by the history being made around them. That's Scottish wifies for you though, they take everything in their stride.

On the personal side, a great big thank you to Lorna, for listening to the stories, checking the manuscript, and her diplomacy in offering such comments "the book is really coming on now, it's great. Between chapters though, do you think you might just give the fridge a wee wipe before it causes a national health and safety alert". Every person who sits down to write a book needs a Lorna.

Introduction

'O hold your tongue of your weeping', said he
'Of your weeping now let me be
I will show you how the lilies grow
On the banks of Italy.

And aye when she turn'd her round about
Aye taller he seem'd for to be
Until the tops o' that gallant ship
Nae taller were than he.

The clouds grew dark and the wind grew loud
And the levin fill'd her e'e
And waesome wail'd the snaw-white sprites
Upon the gurlie sea.

He strack the tap-mast wi' his hand
The foremast wi' his knee
And he brake that gallant ship in twain
And sank her in the sea.

The Scots have always been a nation quick to sing, to celebrate the heroic and believe in the supernatural. This ballad, originating in Aberdeen in the early seventeenth century, tells of a sailor returning to his old love and persuading her to leave her family and run away to sea with him. When she embarks upon his ship, she realises it is an illusion, a trick to entice her on to a ghostly vessel that will take her on a voyage to the bottom of the sea.

Ballads, folklore, and myths were passed down from mother to daughter in the oral tradition, as were recipes and formulas for herbal remedies. Fey-folk or supernatural beings were said to inhabit Caledonia's snow-covered mountains, ancient castles and mysterious glens. On special days, such as the May Day festival or Halloween, the fairy aristocracy were thought to mix with living witches, necromancers and sorcerers. Healing by spells and potions was an accepted part of a colourful Celtic past that grew out of the country's pre-Christian origins.

At this time no one persecuted witches. They were as invulnerable as fairies and saints. If you were clever, then you bribed the local witch with a little milk and honey. No doubt many an old woman with basic knowledge of herbal remedies and an eye to the main chance enjoyed a free meal. However, at the end of the fifteenth century, witchcraft was condemned by Pope Innocent VIII as heresy in several papal bulls and became a capital offence. This inspired two German professors of theology, Jakob Sprenger and Heinrich Kramer, to publish their own guide to witch-hunting in 1486. The *Malleus Maleficarum* ('hammer of the witches'), listed an extensive number of atrocities to be inflicted on suspected witches in order to obtain a confession. The book became the witchfinders' bible, as the feeble-minded, herbalists, and even midwives were persecuted across Europe.

Not only witches were believed to be sources of evil in late sixteenth century Scotland, there was also the 'Scarlet Woman of the Book of Revelations' – the Catholic Church. At that time, a large number of supposedly intelligent men of all classes were discontented with the religious environment in which they lived and the corruption within the Catholic Church in particular. On 11 May 1559 John Knox, a follower of John Calvin's radical teachings, preached a sermon 'vehement against idolatry' in the Church of St John the Baptist in Perth. Knox's diatribe fired up the congregation to go on a rampage, damaging the ornaments and artwork in the church. The men then formed a mob, rushing out of the church to sack the houses of the Grey and Black Friars, and the Carthusian monastery. Many such acts of vandalism took place against Scotland's churches and cathedrals, and many a gentleman added to his personal wealth by 'rescuing' valuable works of art before they were destroyed by the vandals.

Christian Caldwell & Isobel Gowdie: *'Thou Shalt Not Suffer a Witch to Live'*

The new church leaders now emerging were intellectual Scots who had read the works of Luther and Calvin and seen at first-hand the way foreign authorities treated the threat from witches. The persecution of witches suited the politics of their new regime very well. Making witchcraft an illegal act provided a lever against their opponents and helped establish the new religion in the eyes of the people. The Acta Parliamentorum Mariae was passed in 1563, imposing the death penalty on all those practising witchcraft and necromancy. The reformers supported their cause by quoting from Exodus, xxii, 18, 'thou shalt not suffer a witch to live'.

In a society ruled by such a patriarchal and misogynous church it is perhaps hardly surprising that most of those accused of witchcraft were vulnerable women on the margins of society, the wives of craftsmen, farmers, cottars or poor, old widows. Most of those accused in front of the Kirk Session (church court) confessed after being interrogated. A 'brodder' or witch-pricker, was brought in at an early stage of the proceedings to find the devil's mark on their skin. The suspect was stripped, sometimes shaved, and had a metal probe pushed deep into their body. The brodder was usually able to find a mark, as most people suffered from flea bites and blemishes such as warts, moles or bruises.

The brodder was always male and also often a local minister, but this did not deter Christian Caldwell from applying for the job. No records survive to explain why she wanted to join that most despicable of trades, but on 5 March 1662 she posed as John Dicksone, Burgess of Forfar and initialled a contract with the shire of Moray to reside in the county for one year to examine those accused of witchcraft. Perhaps frustrated by the lack of opportunities available to a woman in a male-dominated society, Christian cross-dressed in order to obtain independence and economic power. The salary she was to be paid as the local witch-pricker, six shillings a day and six pounds for every guilty individual she identified, must have been very tempting indeed.

How Christian's true identity was discovered we may never know, but on 30 August 1662 she was interrogated in Edinburgh on charges of false accusation, torture and causing the death of innocent people in Moray – in fact doing her job. Few witch-prickers, if any, were brought to trial over their deeds, which suggests that the undated indictment brought against Christian, that she 'did conterfoot [her] sex [and] took on the habit of a man' was considered to be the more serious offence. Cross-dressing was stepping over the threshold of common decency, challenging the male right to supremacy.

After the witch-pricker found the mark, a suspect was tortured in the tolbooth in order to obtain a confession. There were various forms of torture to choose from. Sleep deprivation was the most popular, but there were many other methods of persuasion. A scold's bridle, or iron-framed headpiece, could be padlocked in place so that it would pierce the roof of the victim's mouth if they attempted to speak. The pilliwinks, or thumbscrews, crushed the thumbs, while the boot, a wooden contraption was designed to crush the leg. All of these techniques were effective in persuading the most stubborn prisoners to confess. A confession having been tortured and beaten out of the accused, she would appear at the next Kirk Session. These appearances gave the illusion that the prisoner was receiving a hearing. Next, the parish minister would approach the civil authorities, who would in turn apply to the Privy Council in Edinburgh for permission to try the case locally. Few witchcraft suspects tried locally escaped the death penalty, as the trials were usually officiated over by those as biased and ignorant as the person who had reported the accused in the first place.

The majority of executions coincided with outbreaks of plague or famine. At a conservative estimate, 4,400 people were executed between 1560 and1680.

In Europe no class was exempt from the witch-hunt, but in Scotland the landed gentry and wealthiest burgesses were seldom accused. No Calvinist wanted to cross swords with one of the country's powerful earls. Due to the ministers' long and ranting sermons on personal demons, descriptions of hell fire, dreadful

The Number of 'Witches' Executed in Scotland (1560–1662)
(Source: *The Scottish Review, October 1891*)

First 30 years of the Reformation (1560–90)	50 witches per annum (total c.1,000)
First epidemic 1590–97	50 witches per annum (350)
Second epidemic 1640–50	100 witches per annum (1,000)
Third epidemic 1660–62	150 witches per annum (450)

warnings and lectures on predestination (the idea that God had already chosen the elect who would go to heaven), some simple rural churchgoers became deluded that they actually were Satanists. Most confessions were obtained under terrible torture, but some women surrendered themselves voluntarily, whilst gripped by the hallucinations these powerful sermons often evoked.

Isobel Gowdie of Nairn confessed to, amongst other things, belonging to a coven of 13 who met for feasting and cursing, having been magically flown down to earth to dine with the King and Queen of the fairies, and making her local minister ill by swinging a bag of boiled toads and nail parings over his bed. She also admitted to being beaten and raped by the Devil in the form of either a stag or bull, or 'a very mickle, black rough man'. In fact, there was no evidence that the minister had suffered any illness at all, but it made no impact on the hysteria instigated by this highly unlikely story. Whilst awaiting execution, Isobel admitted to the lawyer Sir George Mackenzie that she had not confessed because she was guilty, but because having been defamed for a witch, she knew she would starve. She claimed, 'no person thereafter would give her meat or lodgings; therefore she desired to be out of the world'. This confidence may well have been a fabrication on the part of the lawyer to discourage others from pleading their innocence, but Scotland's witches had come a long way from the old herbalist ready to play to the gallery for a free bowl of oats and milk.

Although victims of persecution themselves, it was the Covenanters who were responsible for the witchcraft epidemic of 1640–50. The General Assembly passed several acts in the 1640s, designed to reform the country by searching out witches and destroying them. It seems having been hounded, oppressed and tormented yourself does not stop you victimizing others.

Isabel Alison & Marion Harvie: *The Grassmarket Martyrs*

On 28 February 1638, the National Covenant was signed in front of the pulpit of Greyfriars Church, the signatories choosing Presbyterianism over Anglicanism as the national religion of Scotland. The graveyard surrounding the church would in 1679 become Britain's first recorded concentration camp, when around 12,000 Covenanting men, women and children were herded into the squalor of its confines.

In 1638 Charles I promised to honour the Covenant, only to go back on his word later. The signing of this document precipitated financial ruin for the English monarch and, ultimately, the English Civil War. The restoration of Charles II to the throne in 1660 began the Covenanters' period of martyrdom. The Covenanting armies fought the crown and the Covenant was declared illegal. For the following 25 years the signatories would be brutally persecuted.

Presbyterianism was not the only problematic religion Charles II had to contend with. His brother the Duke of York (later James VII of Scotland, II of England) held views on restoring Catholicism that were fiercely opposed in England. Charles wanted York out of England and sent him to Scotland, creating a position for him as 'His Majesty's Commissioner'. York imposed a tyranny upon the Scottish people that was calculated to subjugate them and, by his own reasoning, eventually convert England to Catholicism. He found a perfect tool in the lawyer Sir George Mackenzie, also known as 'Bloody Mackenzie' and later 'The Hanging Judge'.

Although Mackenzie spent his first years as a lawyer protesting against ignorance, superstition and the burning of witches, personal ambition and a thirst for blood caused him to pervert every principle of law and justice in order to condemn those he chose to execute. One famous trick of his was to overawe the jury with his knowledge of the law and threaten to serve a writ of error if they failed to bring in a proper verdict, the verdict suggested by him.

Among the lawyer's victims were Isabel Alison, a single woman from Perth and Marion Harvie, a young maid from Borrowstounness (now Bo'ness). Isabel was accused of having passed remarks on the cruelty soldiers inflicted on the Covenanters and Marion of attending a forbidden field sermon. There was little evidence against them, apart from both admitting to have heard the Cameronian minister Patrick Scargill preach. The Cameronians, a radical group of Puritan Covenanters, publicly renounced their allegiance to Charles II and were especially sought out for persecution. Despite lack of evidence the case was transferred to the criminal court. At their trial the jury alleged that no fact had been proved. Mackenzie angrily replied the women had admitted to treason, one of the advocate's favourite accusations when all else failed, and threatened the jury with a writ.

Isabel Alison and Marion Harvey were both condemned to death by hanging at the Grassmarket in Edinburgh on 26 January 1681. The sentence was carried out in a manner that was calculated to impose maximum humiliation on the two women. They were hanged alongside three women accused of infanticide, so they would be deemed to be as worthless as the mob judged their fellow sufferers to be. As the two martyrs were led to the scaffold, John Paterson, the Bishop of Edinburgh, tried to drown out their last words by having one of his own curates give a devotional service.

According to an account recorded within *The Scots Worthies* (1830), with great dignity Marion turned to her companion and said "Come Isabel, let us sing the twenty-third psalm". The pair sang psalms and prayed on the scaffold with such fervour that the curate could not be heard. Both were prepared to meet their death, not with resignation, but with triumph. In her final speech Marion condemned the Anglican religion that had brought her to the scaffold with false accusations of treason. The officer of the guard cut her last testimony short by commanding the hangman to give her up. She was promptly strangled with the rope.

After Judge George Mackenzie died in May 1691, his body was conveyed to Greyfriars Churchyard with all pomp and ceremony, only to be buried in the middle of the Covenanters' Prison, where so many of his victims had perished.

During the 1650s, witchcraft trials were all but prohibited by the English government, and during the early 1660s the Scottish authorities too, were beginning to experience revulsion at the witch-hunts, so successful trials became rare after 1680. By the turn of the eighteenth century they were hardly known at all, and it was not the Kirk, nor the Privy Council, that instigated mass anti-witchcraft hysteria in Paisley during the late 1690s, but a spoilt and spiteful 11-year-old girl.

Christian Shaw: *The Bargarran Imposter*

Christian Shaw was the daughter of the wealthy owner of Bargarran, a large estate near Paisley. She was a child prone to tantrums and vindictive retaliation if she did not get her own way, as one of the family's servants, Katherine Campbell discovered to her cost in 1696. She scolded the child over stealing a cup of milk and was rewarded with more than just a fit of hysterics. Five days after the incident Christian's parents heard her screaming in the middle of the night and found her clinging to the walls of her bedroom in a state of extreme terror. She was shouting gibberish and became insensible before fainting at her father's feet. After she regained consciousness, Christian thrashed around, complaining of violent pains and local doctors were summoned.

Even an eminent physician, Dr Brisbane, was at a loss to discover what was causing the ailment. However, there was an easy explanation at hand: Christian accused Katherine Campbell and several other family servants of causing her illness. With a little help from the devil himself, she claimed, these servants had turned into invisible demons in order to torment her. Finally the doctor was able to form a diagnosis – Christian had been bewitched. Christian spat and pulled lumps of hair from her mouth claiming that her invisible tormentors were forcing them down her throat. The doctor decided the condition was not medical but one that required the attention of the Church.

Concerned Kirk elders watched the girl pull straw, hay, cinders, feathers and wool from her mouth and concluded that this was indeed a serious case of sorcery. Lord Balantyne, the head of the Privy Council, conducted an enquiry and Christian faced her alleged tormentors: Katherine Campbell, Agnes Naismith, Margaret Lang, Martha Semple, and John and James Lindsay, as well as Jean Fulton and three of her grandchildren. As soon as the girl set eyes on her former servants she complained of agonies like a swarm of bees attacking her legs and revealed scratches and swellings under her stockings, which she claimed were caused by the accused. After the witch-pricker finished his job, seven of the accused were found to bear the Devil's mark. One of them was acquitted, while James Lindsay took his own life in prison. Five of those found guilty were hanged before a baying crowd in 1697 and thrown, some while still alive, onto a bonfire in the middle of Paisley Green.

Christian was to later admit it had all been a hoax and in 1839 two writers visiting the Shaw estate found a concealed hole next to where her bed had lain, which could easily have concealed shavings and hair. Although now known as the 'Bargarran Imposter', Christian was never brought to account for the five cases of judicial murder and one suicide she contrived to bring about, and the bereaved families did not receive compensation in any form. In 1719 Christian married the Reverend John Millar, Minister of Kilmaurs. When her husband died two years later, she worked with her mother and sister at the Bargarran Thread Company. The women bleached yarn to produce strong white thread, which was marketed under the family coat of arms and became the basis for the Paisley cotton industry. It seems that she retired from business on marrying William Livingstone, a glover, in 1737. We will never know whether or not her past followed her.

Mary Macleod & Cecily MacDonald: *The Highland Poetesses*

The Reformed Church, or Presbyterian Church as it became, was a profound influence not only on individual lives but on the cultural growth of Scotland. A great leap forward was accomplished in sixteenth and seventeenth century Europe, with the intellectual and artistic achievements of men like Descartes, Locke, Rubens, Rembrandt, and Shakespeare all within this period. In Scotland, George Buchanan, tutor to the young James VI achieved recognition with his Latin composition, poems and dramatic tragedies, while John Napier of Merchiston was known as a litigious laird and an eccentric inventor.

In the closing decades of the seventeenth century, Sir Robert Sibbald laid the foundations of the country's reputation for excellence in medical education by beginning the first investigation into the natural history of fish, birds, plants and whales and founding the botanical gardens at Edinburgh as a herbarium around 1667. But some of the greatest Scottish achievements between 1560 and 1690 were those in the vernacular art of poetry. Building on the tradition of the medieval ballad-makers and the 'makars' of the court circle, poets like Dunbar, Lyndsay and Douglas produced some of Scotland's finest works. The ballads and verse that emerged were born of an economy of narration and images of beauty and eeriness.

The development of Scottish poetry received a setback with the union of the crowns in 1603 and the removal of the Holyrood court to London. A new generation of Lowland poets abandoned the versatility of their own tongue for verse written in standard English. With the signing of the Covenant by Charles I in 1638, the Covenanting puritans struck the greatest blow to the development of Scottish literature. For almost a century, hardly a line of good verse was penned by a Lowland Scot. Instead, all offerings revolved around the sufferings of Restoration Covenanters and amounted to little more than doggerel.

Meanwhile, poetry written in Gaelic was flourishing. In the seventeenth century the Highland Bards reached new cultural heights, led by the Highland poetesses. Around 1600, at the court of the MacLeods, male poets, the MacCrimmons devised the Piobaireachd (Pibroch), the art of Highland piping still popular today. Yet it was a female member of the Dunvegan court who wrote some of the most beautiful songs of the period. Mary MacLeod (Mairi Nighean Alasdair Ruaidh MacLeod) was born in 1615 to Sibella Mackenzie and John MacLeod, who was descended from the fifth chief of the MacLeods.

During Mary's lifetime there was great Gaelic poetic activity in Scotland and Ireland. Between 1645 and 1725 the Gaelic Bards, a group of around 50, led by Mary MacLeod and Iain Lom, developed a similar outlook in style and thought. Especially remarkable for their talents were the poetesses Dorothy Brown, Selena Ceapaich and Mairead Nighean Laichlainn, who, like Mary MacLeod, flourished in this period, composing some of the most beautiful of all Gaelic songs. Mary's poetry and songs were originally known only through the oral tradition and they were not written down until the eighteenth century. Her writing incorporates a large amount of the imagery of the Bardic poets and is mostly involved with the heroic exploits of the MacLeod family for whom she had a deep emotional affection.

Although losing some of its magic in the English translation, Mary's songs like this one, with its echo of the Song of Solomon, are still beautiful:

Roderick, Roderick,
Roderick of yonder dun,
Thou art my mirth
and my merry music,
Thou art my rosary
and the comb of my hair
Though art my fruit-garden
Wherein are apples …

A nurse taking care of her chief's children, Mary's first song was written to entertain her charges. Later, she is said to have displeased her chief with one of her songs and was banished to the Isle of Mull. She was allowed to return upon the condition that she composed no more literary pieces challenging her chief's authority. As was typical of bards at the time, Mary's compositions were often satirical or even obscene. The true story behind her exile may never be known as Mary's life story, like her songs was not documented but passed down in the oral tradition.

An even more outspoken poetess than Mary MacLeod was Cicely MacDonald, or Sileas Nighean Mhic Raghnail, born around 1660 to Mary Cameron or MacMartin, and Guilleasbuig, Chief of the MacDonalds of Keppoch. A member of the higher strata of Gaelic society, she became a bard in the classic style, composing elegies on the deaths of those important to her. Many of those beautiful short pieces became models for future Gaelic songs. As a Roman Catholic, Cicely was an enemy of Protestantism and used a great deal of her muse to protest against the house of Hanover. She was fiercely opposed to the Acts of Union in 1707, and in one of her earliest poems, she described the union as a *'uinneian punnsein'* (a poisoned onion) served up to the Scots.

Cecily would gain a reputation for being coarse and indelicate for two of her songs, 'Comhairle air na Nigheanan Oga' (Advice to Young Girls) and 'An aghaidh na h-Obair Nodha' (Against the New Work). The first song gives young girls advice on sexual morality, using Cicely's own experiences as a guideline against falling for the flattery of young men. Biographies have described her as 'frolicsome' and the work suggests that during the mid-1680s she gave birth to a child before she married Gordon of Camdell. Gordon was to die from a fit of intoxication whilst on a visit to Inverness.

Cecily's second notorious song, her protest against 'The New Work', a response to a poem by MacKenzie of Gruineard in which he praises sexual licence in explicit terms, describes the abandonment, pregnancy and disgrace girls would have to face if they succumbed to MacKenzie's new brand of immorality. Due to her standing in the Gaelic community, Cicely seems to have received little more than a mild rebuke from her peers for challenging the wisdom of the male poet.

Cuckolds and Chastity Belts

Despite the dissolving of teaching at the song schools, where the Catholic clergy had trained boys, musical performances continued for several decades after the Reformation. Music was played in private homes throughout the seventeenth century and actively encouraged in religious services. Much was made of turning profane songs into sacred pieces. Dramatic performances continued until after 1574, when only plays under Royal protection were staged and the Presbyterian Church discouraged performances on the grounds that they fostered licence and superstition. Modern drama emerging in the Renaissance period was rooted in the various folk, religious and courtly activities. Thirteenth century church records reveal the church attempting to ban shameful games and plays within its precincts.

One such folk ceremony, to celebrate spring, was recorded in 1282 within the *Chronicle of Lanercost* (a Franciscan record of Scottish life between 1201 and 1346). John, a priest of the Fife parish of Inverkeithing, had been celebrating the profane rites of Priapus by gathering together the little girls of the town, forming them into a circle to honour Father Bacchus, and instructing them to dance in an immodest manner. The bystanders claimed to 'be incited to lust' when John carrying a large phallus on a stick began to dance around them using crude miming and profane language. Apparently the church received a few complaints.

Ane Satyre of the Thrie Estaitis, a drama written by Sir David Lyndsay, the son of a Fife laird, heralded in the Reformation and is regarded as one of the greatest of Scottish plays. Lyndsay's writing often expressed sixteenth century attitudes towards women of both high and low birth, and the play was a farce written to celebrate the arrival of James V's new queen Mary of Guise at St Andrews. It contains a line dedicated to her 'quhilk teichit hir to serve hir God, obey hir husband and keep hir body clene according to Godi's will and commandement'. We can only wonder how these instructions were received by Mary of Guise, who went on to become an able and shrewd regent during the minority of her daughter, Mary Queen of Scots. The play was first performed at the feast of Epiphany on 6 January 1540, before James V and the Scottish court in the Great Hall at Linlithgow Palace. *The Thrie Estaitis* also satirised the sensuality and greed of the clergy, implying that the Catholic Church was badly in need of reforming.

By 1552, the play was preceded by an advertisement, a short play in itself called *The Cupar Proclamation,* a farce made up of separate cameos and drawn from stock comedy characters. An old man is cuckolded by his young wife, Bessy. She is offered fine clothes and gold by her admirers and in order to keep her for himself, he locks her in a chastity belt then hides the key under his head whilst he is sleeping. Bessy is not interested in those wealthy admirers, but she is keen on the fool of the play, because he has a big penis ('the best that evir ye saw'). The fool removes the key from under the sleeping husband, who has no idea that he is being cuckolded.

Other characters include a henpecked husband and his quick-fisted wife trading insults. He tells her, 'Besyd you nane may stand for stink'. For the new Queen, Lyndsay writes 'teach her to keep her body clean according to God's will' yet for the farmer's wife 'Nobody stinks like you' suffices. Although women in general had little say in the running of their lives, some were shown more respect than others.

Sir David Lyndsay also had some advice for those women attending the play who would have to wait four hours until its conclusion: 'Faill nocht to teme your bleddir [empty your bladder]', otherwise 'some of yow sall mak ane richt wait sark [a wet shirt]'. It was good advice.

Part One

1690–1800

Chapter One

Wives – A Valuable Commodity

In a wee cot hoose far across the muir,
Where pease-weeps, plovers, an' waups cry dreary,
There liv'd an auld maid for mony lang years,
Wha ne'er a woo-er did e'er ca her dearie,
A lanely lass was Kate Dalrymple,
A thrifty quean was Kate Dalrymple,
Nae music, exceptin' the clear burnie's wimple,
Was heard round the dwellin' o' Kate Dalrymple

Her face had a smack o' the gruesome an' grim
That did frae the fash o' a' the wooers defend her
Her long Roman nose nearly met wi' her chin,
That brang folk in mind o' the auld witch o' Endor
A wiggle in her walk had Kate Dalrymple
A sniggle in her talk had Kate Dalrymple
An' mony a cornelian an' Cairngorm pimple
Did blaze on the dun face of Kate Dalrymple

But mony are the ups an' the downs in life,
When the dice-box o' fates jumbled a' tapsal-teerie,
Sae Kate fell heiress to a rich frien's estate,
An' nae langer for woo-ers had she cause to weary
The Laird came a-wooin' soon o' Kate Dalrymple
The lawyer, scrapin', bowin', fan oot Kate Dalrymple;
Owre ilk woo-ers face was seen love's smilin' dimple,
Sae noo she's nae mair Kate but Miss Dalrymple'.

(Traditional Scottish Reel by William Watt
on society beauty, Grace Dalrymple Elliot)

Scotland's two best-known female celebrities lived centuries apart and came from totally different walks of life, yet both achieved fame due to the extensive documentation of their lives. The privileged but tragic life of Mary Queen of Scots is preserved in Scotland's archives. The existence of the famous 'Casket Letters', her adultery and accusations of complicity in the murder of her husband Henry Stuart, Lord Darnley have all been discussed and disputed in numerous biographies, and her life continues to be a matter for both academic interest and speculation.

Meanwhile, born fully-formed in Glebe Street in 1936, Maw Broon was the creation of cartoonist Dudley Watkins and Robert Low, a managing editor at D.C. Thomson. The brood Maw presides over – her husband Paw, her old rogue of a father-in-law Grandpaw, bookish son Horace, glamorous daughter Maggie, plain Daphne, attractive Joe, lanky Hen, the twins and the bairn – are not only a family but a fair representation of society at the time. Maw is iconic in that she is not only the family matriarch but mother to all working-class Scots. Up until the last few decades, Maw Broon stood for all that was considered admirable in Scottish women. A martyr to her family's problems and predicaments, she was selfless and dependable in maintaining their respectability. Committed to shopping, cooking, cleaning and meeting their every need, Maw, and women like her, had no time for any passions or hobbies of their own.

Whether born into sixteenth century royalty or an early twentieth century tenement, one of the major deciding factors in all Scottish women's lives was their choice of husband, or rather the husband who chose them. Both the conniving Lord Darnley and the mischievous Paw Broon dictated the standards by which their wives lived. Only a few women could afford the privilege of staying single. Until the nineteenth century, on marrying a woman lost independent legal status and was considered to come under the authority of her husband. Legal status and financial autonomy was only returned to women when they became widowed. Wealthy widows were considered by some fortune-seekers as desirable wives but many women chose not to remarry and flourished by their own efforts.

On the death of her first husband, Robert Kennedy, a writer who died in 1671, Mary Erskine became a shopkeeper. After the death of her second, an apothecary, she paid off his debts and developed into a successful businesswoman. She was a property owner and wedwife, or moneylender, letting out properties and lending money to businessmen, professionals and to other widows wishing to either continue their husband's business or start their own. Mary did not trust her now considerable wealth in the hands of a third husband, instead becoming a philanthropist. She generously contributed to a proposal for a school to educate the daughters of Edinburgh burgesses and impoverished girls of the city's middle classes. This became the Edinburgh Ladies College, later the Mary Erskine School, which is now one of the oldest schools in the world. Mary also helped to establish the Merchant Maiden Hospital, founded in 1694, as well as bequeathing money to the Incorporations of Trades, who had followed the merchants in setting up their own hospital.

For single women, remaining unmarried could be a risky business. Women living alone or with other women were often suspected of prostitution. In the late Middle Ages it seems that in Scottish cities prostitution was tolerated and controlled, officially confined to brothels. By 1530, magistrates in Edinburgh saw only two prospects for domestic servants dismissed on becoming pregnant – marriage or the brothel. The brothel was seen by some as a place to consign unruly women. After the Scottish Reformation in 1560, the reformers took a different view of such immorality and efforts were made to stamp out prostitution altogether. What had been a frowned upon but legal means for a woman to earn money now became a crime, and its perpetrators were hunted and punished.

Rather than live outside the model household and risk prosecution, there were women who hid behind a marriage as they looked elsewhere for their unconventional sexual pleasures. These women could also come to the attention of the Kirk and the law. Maud Galt was the wife of wright John Dickie, and lived in

Kilbarchan with her husband and two servants. One of her servants, Agnes Mitchell, brought a complaint against her employer at a Kirk Session in September 1649. She brought to the Kirk a piece of clay shaped into the likeness of a man's private member and claimed Maud had done unspeakable things to her with the rudely-shaped clay.

Agnes wanted to take the complaint to the local laird, but was hindered by the shame of the act done to her, which was said to have been witnessed by two neighbours. The session investigated Maud Galt's 'vyle act in abusing ane of hir servants with ane peis [piece] of clay formed lyk the secreit members of ane man', but decided to bring a charge of witchcraft against her instead. There is no record of any commission for Maud's trial, so the charges may have been dropped.

Outlaws and In-laws

Five thousand years ago women held positions of high spiritual power in Scotland. In the Neolithic period communal sharing was phased out in Scotland and agriculture developed. Gradually, land ownership took over and women's lives changed drastically. Society was split between landowners and a hierarchal system of slaves. Mothers lost their spiritual prestige and became regarded as part of a man's property. With the coming of Christianity, female independence declined even further and would change little over the next 1,400 years. Bible teachings thumped home the message that the female sex was morally lacking, it symbolized temptation, corrupted men and needed to be brought under control.

By 1690 the Reformation was complete and Presbyterianism firmly in charge not only of women, but the whole of Scottish society. One of the most difficult customs the reformed church intended to conquer in its quest to control the populace was the rising number of what it considered irregular marriages. At that time, under canon law dating back to the Middle Ages, all that was required for a marriage to be legal was for the bride and groom to state that they would take each other for man and wife in the presence of two witnesses. A promise to marry, followed by sexual intercourse was also regarded as binding if witnesses could confirm that the couple had shared a bed.

One reason for the rise of irregular marriages after the revolution of 1689/90 was the beginning of the reign of William III and Mary II, after the Roman Catholic James VII fled to France. This resulted in a change from Episcopal Church government to the Presbyterian Church and most Episcopal ministers were thrown out of their posts. For a fee, some now penniless ministers would still conduct marriages for those who preferred a ceremony conducted by the Episcopalian clergy. Such marriages were outlawed and could not be legally performed until the Marriage Act of 1711, which allowed only certain Episcopalian ministers to conduct the ceremony. Others, known as celebrators, including some defrocked ministers like David Strang, who was dismissed from a northern parish for misconduct, were happy to marry couples for a small fee.

The cost of a regular wedding and celebration was beyond the means of many couples, and some bridegrooms were soldiers or sailors on leave, wishing to marry before rejoining their regiment or ship. The Church came down hard on all those participating in such marriages. An act was passed in 1661 threatening offenders who married outside the church with three months' imprisonment and a sliding scale of fines from a hundred merks (silver marks) to a thousand Scots pounds. In 1698 a further act also penalised witnesses at such weddings and the men who conducted the ceremony.

The Kirk believed that the proclamation of banns on three successive Sundays and a ceremony carried out by the parish church minister made a wedding a sufficiently public event to deter bigamy. Instead, these new rules often caused the couple financial hardship, as they were required to pay 'consignation money', which was only returned to them if a child was not born less than nine months later and there was no boisterous party after the wedding. To prevent the riotous drinking and dancing that usually took place at the penny weddings or parties held by those who could not afford lavish celebrations, such receptions were forbidden. It is perhaps unsurprising that the less well-off decided to avoid a regular wedding, if they were such dour events!

Changes in marriage trends were not only those brought about by the reformists. In medieval times parents chose marriage partners for their children from local families. Wealthy families gave great thought to the property and status of their daughter's prospective bridegroom. As most people had limited social circles, the girl's wishes usually coincided with those of her parents due to sheer lack of choice. Towards the end of the seventeenth century, however, young girls began to be sent off to boarding school and allowed to attend balls and functions in Edinburgh, where they met young men unknown to their families. Children began to demand a greater say in their choice of marriage partner, but now more than ever money and status mattered most. A connection with an influential family was seen as worthwhile as matrimonial allegiances, between members of the aristocracy had a great deal of influence on politics, legal battles and everyday business.

Some young men were beginning to consider more than just the tocher (dowry), and demanded certain personal qualities in their brides. A pious young woman of impeccable reputation, who was also frugal in controlling her household budget, was the ideal life-partner. Virtue was important to a man, and equally an honourable husband was valued by most women, so all the rules of etiquette had to be observed during the courtship. If the first meeting between the prospective couple was a success, then the gentlemen would call upon the family and write regularly to the young woman. Girls were not allowed to take the initiative.

When everything was settled to the mutual satisfaction of the couple and their families, the marriage contract was drawn up. Many contracts began with a promise of marriage between the two signatories and the date of the wedding, though this was often left blank as a fine could be imposed if there was a delay. The main issues of the contract to be settled were the size of the jointure, the piece of land put in joint possession of bride and groom, and the tocher, or dowry. The wife did not directly draw any financial benefits from this land, but during her husband's lifetime she would be supported by him. If the husband predeceased his wife, she could draw an annuity for her maintenance. The tocher was usually for a larger sum than the value of the land and again came under the control of the husband. With all the bargaining completed, the wedding would take place the day after the banns were read for the third time. In prosperous families the celebrations could last for several weeks, supported by a vast supply of beef, freshly-baked bread, sweetmeats and wine. Marriage contracts were not only exchanged between members of the aristocracy and landed gentry, but also amongst more humble members of society. Only the amount of money involved and what was to be gained by both parties varied.

Most of the middle classes in urban areas of Scotland once belonged to the mercantile professions and guilds. A man would normally enter the mercantile profession as a teenage apprentice and on finishing his training qualify to become a burgess and enter the appropriate guild. There were several ways to gain membership: as the son of a merchant; paying a hefty fee; waiting a further period of time; or the option most young men preferred, marrying the daughter of their master or another merchant. The possession of such a wife gave the apprentice not only inexpensive entry into the guild, but it also provided a small tocher and the seal of complete respectability. For the merchant it was a cheap way of disposing of the daughter whilst securing some guarantee that he would be cared for by a well set up mercantile family in his old age. Farmers, weavers, millers, dyers and servants all made marriage contracts following the fashions of the peerage. The settlements may have been smaller, yet just as much thought went into the process. Only the penniless could afford to marry for love.

Honeymoons, or honeymonths, were popular, but the bride and groom did not go away together. Instead the wedding night was generally spent at the home of the bride's parents. If the couple wished for a little privacy after their nuptials, then they would be sorely disappointed. The public bedding of the pair was part of the entertainment. The last part of the marriage ritual was the homecoming, when bride and groom left the celebrations to set up home together. They were accompanied by the wedding guests and the first feast of the new home was held. It was usually well into the night before the last guest left these lavish affairs

Jean Cochrane: *Sealed With a Curse*

While the marriage expectations of both parents and offspring often coincided, there were naturally exceptions, and no choice of husband could have created a bigger conflict between mother and daughter than the one made by Jean Cochrane in 1684. Jean was the daughter of William Cochrane, who predeceased his father, also William, the 1st Earl of Dundonald. By the time Jean reached a marriageable age, her grandfather was old and feeble and her widowed mother, a staunch supporter of the Covenanters, was the dominant presence in the household. It was a divided family, the elderly Earl of Dundonald having supported the Stuarts.

Lady Cochrane's choice of husband for her only daughter was Henry Pollock, a Covenanting minister. Pollock had been born into a Cavalier and Episcopalian family, but after being enchanted by the sermons of the preachers Rutherford and Blair, he decided to join the Covenanters in the west of Scotland. When Charles II was restored to the throne, Pollock found the misrule and brutality inflicted upon the Scottish people sickening, and left for Holland to study theology, before being ordained as a Presbyterian Church minister. On hearing Pollock's declaration of love for her daughter, Lady Cochrane encouraged him to propose. Jean had become critical of her mother's Covenanting ways, but as the ruler of her household, Lady Cochrane was determined to put down her daughter's rebellion.

Jean kindly, but firmly, refused Pollock. Her own choice of husband was John Graham of Claverhouse, 1st Viscount Dundee.

Graham was known as 'Bluidy Clavers' to the Presbyterians and 'Bonnie Dundee' to those who supported the Jacobites, as he hunted the Covenanters on behalf of James VII. Graham found himself besotted by Jean Cochrane, but remembering her ancestry and his cause, he decided it would be an unsuitable match. According to legend, the old Earl sent a message to Graham asking to see him, and on this visit he ran into Jean in the courtyard. He proposed and was accepted. Both agreed that the sooner they were married the better.

Lord Dundonald was pleased with the match, but the news sent Lady Cochrane into a blind fury. She is said to have strode through the rooms of Paisley Castle, accusing her daughter of disgracing the family's good name and giving herself into the hands of the Kirk's cruellest enemy. After the marriage contract was signed by Lord Dundonald and Jean's grandmother, the old countess, the wedding took place in the castle's gallery. Officiating was a minister who had taken the indulgence (indulged in alcohol), and was given a wide berth by the stricter members of the Kirk. Lady Cochrane was not invited, but apparently managed to hide herself in an alcove. When the minister asked if anyone could show just cause for why the marriage should not be performed, she revealed herself, saying, "I the mother of Jean Cochrane, forbid this marriage, because she is marrying against my will, and joining herself to the persecutor of God's people, because she is turning herself against her father's house and forsaking the faith of her father's God".

The minister, uncertain whether or not to continue, looked to Jean. "I have made my choice," Jean declared and Claverhouse nodded for the service to go on. After the ceremony was completed and Graham kissed his bride, there was a moment of silence before Lady Cochrane spoke again:

> "*Ye have gone your own way and done your own will, John Graham and Jean Cochrane, and the curse of God's kirk and of a mother goes with you. The veil is lifted before my eyes and I prophesy that neither*

> *the bridegroom nor the bride will die in their beds. There are those here present who will witness one day that I have spoken true."*

After the church service, Graham had to depart. Two days before the wedding news had come that there was a rising among the Covenanters and his regiment was waiting in the town for him to pursue them. His saddled horse stood in the courtyard. Jean's honeymoon was spent with her mother at Paisley Castle, as she waited for Graham to return and take her to his castle situated above the town of Dundee. Temporarily reprieved from his duties hunting Covenanters, Graham was given the office of Provost of Dundee and the pair were able to take up residence at Dudhope Castle. Neither Jean nor Graham was popular in the town. Ordinary people thought Graham a persecutor and Jean a renegade. Men turned away their faces as they passed her in the streets and women shouted 'Bluidy Clavers' after her. Despite this, the marriage appears to have been a happy one.

When once more Graham was sent in search of the Covenanters he wrote to Jean from Edinburgh:

> *Sweetheart,*
>
> *It is my one trouble when I must leave you, and save when I am engaged on the king's work my every thought is with you, for indeed it appeareth to me that if I loved you with strong desire on the day of our marriage, I love you more soul and body this day … When the night cometh, and the task of the day is done, I hold you in my embrace, the proudest woman in Scotland, and you say again, as on that day in the pleasaunce, "For Life, John Graham, and for death" [English Translation].*

In the same letter, Graham goes on to give Jean news of her first suitor Henry Pollock:

> *Mayhap you have heard … that we lighted upon Henry Pollock and a party of his people last week. They were going to some preaching and were taken unawares, and we captured them all, not without blows and*

> *blood. Pollock himself fought as ye might expect … We brought him on horseback to Edinburgh, treating him as well as we could … I do not forget that he loved you. Yesterday he was tried before the Council and I gave strong evidence against him … This morning he was executed and since there was a fear lest the people who have greatly loved him should attempt to rescue, I was present with two troops of horse. It needeth not me to tell you that he died well.*

Pollock's death was Claverhouse's doing. A staunch supporter of Charles II and later his brother James VII, John Graham joined the Jacobites. He led the rebel Highland army against King William's commander, General Hugh Mackay, at the Battle of Killiecrankie on 27 July 1689. Although the rebel army won the fight, Graham was killed on the battlefield. His last words were reported to have been for Jean. After Graham's death, Jean married William Livingstone, 3rd Viscount of Kilsyth and gave him a son. In 1695, whilst the family were visiting a house in Holland, the turf roof collapsed. Although Livingstone was pulled clear, Jean, the boy and his nurse were killed. Lady Cochrane's curse was complete.

Chapter Two

Fornication, Adultery and Divorce

They next opened his vest, to give him air, when to the great astonishment of all present, the handsome young footman was discovered to be a female. On being restored to consciousness, she related the story of her past life, to the great mirth of the whole wedding party; but as may be expected, it was a great disappointment to the newly made wife, Miss Wilson …

McDonald assumed her proper character, and wishes to join in wedlock with a suitable young man, with £100. One about to go to Australia would be preferred …

(Broadsheet, 'The Life and Strange Adventures of Margaret M'Donald The Female Foot Boy', National Library of Scotland)

Under the old Catholic Church, in most cases priests would turn a blind eye to the misdemeanours of the general population. Usually, a private confession between priest and sinner was considered penance enough. The case of Janet Bruce in 1547 was rare. Janet's priest told her to go into Edinburgh High Street and give a chaplain a wax candle, then seek out Isobel Carrington. In front of three witnesses and in good Scots, Janet was to admit to Isobel that she had wrongfully accused her of being a 'bluidy whore'. She also had to apologize to Robert, Isobel's husband for calling him a cuckold, when she knew that his wife was an honest woman. Then Janet would admit she did not know for a fact that Isobel had copulated with an 'auld official', and Isobel would forgive her. Such public apologies were ordered to reconcile the arguing parties, rather than punish them.

With the Reformation of 1560 came a new civil society, which ordered every event of daily life. New courts and laws came into practice and with them new crimes. John Knox and his followers were determined to stamp out each and every incident of raucous behaviour throughout the nation. Adultery and witchcraft were banned in 1563, followed by fornication in 1567, then the wearing of fashionable dress and swearing in 1581. Curfews were imposed on the citizens of Edinburgh too. Theatre performances, carnivals and processions were banned with some success, while restrictions on prostitution and drunkenness failed miserably.

Before the Reformation, divorce could only be sought through the ecclesiastical courts on the grounds of one partner's adultery. The reformers, keen to condemn adultery, made it a crime punishable by death under the 1563 Act. There is no record of any adulterer being executed, yet few would have wished to be cited as an adulterer in the commissary court where divorce cases were now heard. The reformers also extended grounds for divorce to include wilful desertion, when the deserted spouse could prove both the marriage and desertion.

Only 35 divorce cases were recorded in Scotland during the years 1656 to 1707, and these occurred mainly in Edinburgh. These cases included not only the wealthy upper classes, but the middle classes and professionals too. Nineteen were raised by the wife, as opposed to 15 brought by the husband. From the successful applications, it would seem women were given a fair hearing, although they could not personally argue their case. Procurators were appointed on behalf of women, and lawyers used the opportunity to earn a substantial fee.

Although an uncontested divorce could be finalised in three months, the costs of legal action meant that divorce was out of the question for the majority of feuding couples. Also various problems within a marriage could not be solved by divorce. For instance, it was impossible to dissolve the marriage on the grounds of cruelty, and many distressing cases of domestic violence were not brought to the attention of the courts. The best an abused wife could do in these circumstances was to seek a judicial separation. In cases where nothing could be proved against the husband, many judges were still sympathetic.

John Dawling of Leith was among those husbands whose cruelty towards their wives was exposed in court. The council heard that Dawling attacked his wife, Jean Lyon (married women kept their own surname until the nineteenth century), in one of Edinburgh's crowded streets. Dawling had punched and trampled on Jean 'as if she had been a very dog' and the council considered his behaviour 'to be a great crime'. Dawling was ordered to stay away from his wife and to pay her 600 merks a year for her upkeep. If he threatened or molested Jean again, the judge warned that he would receive a heavy prison sentence.

Lady Rachel Grange: *The Bride Packed a Pistol*

The law could offer no remedy for mental cruelty and there were certain marital difficulties that could only be resolved by one partner taking the law into their own hands. The turbulent marriage of Rachel Chiesley and James Erskine, Lord Grange, during the early eighteenth century, reveals the lengths some went to.

After a period of debauchery as a law student, James Erskine, Lord Grange, met Rachel Chiesley and the pair embarked on an affair, during which Grange repeatedly promised to marry her. Grange's family were not in favour of the match; they considered Rachel an unsuitable wife for a rising young lawyer. She also came from a scandalous family. In 1680, angry after having lost a lawsuit, Rachel's father had assassinated the presiding judge as he left the Court of Session. Ambitious and cautious, Grange hesitated to make wedding plans. As legend has it, only when the prospective bride threatened him with a pistol did he keep his promise to marry her.

Lady Grange was a passionate woman given to violent rages, and Grange a man fond of womanising, drinking and swearing. The marriage started well enough, as Grange took up religion and learned to curb his excesses. Four sons and five daughters were born to the couple between 1709 and 1717, but some years later their real troubles began. Rachel's behaviour became so unpredictable that her children began to fear her and she became obsessed with the idea that her husband kept a mistress in London. This may not have been true, however there were rumours that Lord Grange was having a long-standing affair with a handsome Scotswoman, Fanny Lindsay, who kept a coffee house in the Haymarket, Edinburgh.

Such was her obsession with her husband's infidelity that Lady Grange began to make life a misery for everyone around her. She stalked her husband wherever he went, abused him in public, swore at his relations and terrorized her household. In a bid to pacify and distract her, Grange made his wife the official factor of his estate but she proved so extravagant in her spending that he replaced her, before fleeing to London. Left alone in Edinburgh, Lady Grange screamed and raged, threatening to follow her husband to London and confront him with his evil deeds. She shrieked and cursed, constantly changed her mind about everything and ran around the house in her nightgown, threatening to kill herself. In January 1732, she actually went as far as booking a place on the London coach, yet she never took up her seat.

Late one night, a party of Highlanders burst into her ladyship's bedroom, trussed up, gagged, and blindfolded her, then carried her out to a sedan chair. After a short journey she was lifted out of the chair and placed on a horse behind the rider. She was transported to the deserted Castle Tioram, on Loch Moidart in the West Highlands. From there she was taken to the lonely Hebridean island of Heiskir. After she had been kept prisoner on the island for two years, the family looking after Lady Grange refused to put up with her any longer. She spent the following four years on the remote island of Hirta (one of the islands collectively known as St Kilda), with only a young Gaelic-speaking girl to look after her. Grange explained his wife's disappearance by telling friends and family that she was insane and being held at a place in the Highlands for her own safety. Yet, in 1738 Lady Grange managed to have a letter smuggled to the mainland in which she described her seizure and imprisonment. An expedition set out to rescue her, but by the time the boat arrived she had been moved. After this she was kept in various places on the islands of Skye and Harris until she died in 1745.

Lord and Lady Grange were victims of their conflicting personalities, the marriage laws of the time, and a lack of understanding regarding psychiatric disorders. As emotionally disturbed as she appeared to be, Lady Grange gave her husband no legal grounds for divorce. She did not commit adultery and far from deserting him, she was determined to hold on to him. Had she been able to see their desperate situation more clearly, she might have realised that she could divorce him on the grounds of his adultery and put an end to the family's misery.

Nonetheless, divorce came with its own problems. A husband was supposed to maintain his wife throughout the proceedings. If she had brought a tocher (dowry) to the marriage, then the annual payment would be based on that amount and her property would be divided between them. The difficulty lay in persuading the husband to pay. There were complaints to the Privy Council of many a husband who did not pay his due, either by refusing point blank or because his whereabouts were unknown.

In divorces granted for the wife's adultery, the tocher remained with the husband. If the wife was the guilty party then she forfeited the jointure and lost any claim to her tocher. She was also forbidden to marry the co-respondent in the divorce action (the party she had committed adultery with). Whatever the grounds for divorce, the children remained in the custody of the father, unless he had been proved unfit, or his religious beliefs found unsatisfactory. A divorced wife lost her children, much or all of her income, as well as her male protector, and she faced an uncertain future.

Jean Gordon: *Unto Death Us Do Part*

Some privileged, upper class women endured difficult marriages, but women born into Scotland's under classes could be completely trapped by their father's choice of husband. For such women, divorce was not an option, and as Jean Gordon discovered, in the absence of the husband, then sons would step in to run family life.

Born into one of the gypsy tribes of Kirk Yetholm, a village one mile west of the English border, Jean Gordon would be charged, 62 years later with being 'an Egyptian, common vagabond and notorious thief'. The first reference to the presence of gypsies or 'Egyptians' in Scotland was recorded in 1492, when one Peter Ker was paid four shillings for subscribing letters to the 'King of Rowmais' for James IV. Two days later, the monarch authorized a payment of 20 pounds to be made to a messenger sent by the 'King of Rowmais'. There is no record of what the payment was for.

Records of criminal trials survive from the 1540s onwards, detailing murders and violent incidents concerning the border gypsies. These mostly concerned two prominent Yetholm families: the Baillies and the Faas. The fighting was mainly inter-tribal and the amount of alcohol consumed at the many border fairs often added to the friction. The Yetholm gypsies were fortunate in that those sober enough could vanish over the border and wait for everything to calm down before returning. There were enough herds of wild deer and other animals roaming the Cheviot Hills to sustain them in hiding.

Several Acts were passed by the early seventeenth century, describing 'Egyptians' as vagabonds, common thieves and sorcerers and allowing them to be apprehended on sight and hanged. It was also an offence to harbour a gypsy. This brutal legislation led to the majority of gypsy families changing their names and style of dress, taking care not to speak Romany in public, intermarrying with locals and moving nearer to the English border. Yet, neither the Baillie nor the Faa families changed their name or their habits. The Baillies kept up their tradition of wearing coats of green and scarlet, whilst keeping sporting dogs at their side. The women dressed as ladies, attended fairs riding side-saddle on ponies, leaving servants to care for their children at home.

When the tolbooth at the border town of Haddington became full in 1636, the citizens of the town protested against the continued detention of gypsies. They complained to the Privy Council that holding them there merely encouraged their friends and relatives to remain in the area. The council acknowledged the problem and found the following solution. The Sheriff of Haddington or his deputy would pronounce 'doom and sentence of death against so many of the thieves that are men, and against so many of the thieves that are women as wants children, ordering the men to be hanged and the women drowned; and that such of the women that had children were to be banished from Haddington after being branded on the cheek'.

At nearly six feet tall, with remarkable features and style of dress, Jean Gordon was well-known in the borders, having married Patrick Faa, the first Gypsy King in Kirk Yetholm. Before Patrick was convicted of fire-raising and transported to America in 1714, Jean bore him nine sons. One was to be brutally murdered and the other eight would die on the gallows. Alexander Faa was killed at Huntley Wood in 1727. His murderer, Robert Johnstone, escaped after being sentenced to death but was recaptured and returned to Jedburgh, where he was hanged. By 1730, Jean was to lose five more of her offspring, all to the gallows after either justly being accused of dishonesty or found guilty on trumped-up charges of 'being an evil-doing Gypsy'. In 1730 her remaining three sons and two of their wives were tried at Jedburgh for sheep-stealing. All were found guilty and all were hanged on the same day.

Jean herself apparently tried to live by honest means and disapproved of those who did not. Despite her high moral standards, she was to find herself in court two years after the last of her sons had died on the gallows. She pleaded that she was old and infirm, and had been held in prison a long time. Promising that she would leave the country if released, the court accepted her assurances and she was banished from Scotland forever. For many years Jean wandered the north of England, hankering after Scotland and the Jacobite cause. Whilst in Carlisle during the Jacobite Rebellion in 1746, she foolishly pledged her support for the Young Pretender in front of a Hanoverian mob. The aggrieved crowd dragged Jean to the Eden and drowned her. According to tradition, her last words were "Charlie yet! Charlie yet!"

Airing Your Dirty Linen in Public

It was not only in the divorce courts that women's private lives were exposed to the general public. In the mid-seventeenth century, the Kirk formed a system of interlocking, interdependent ecclesiastical courts, starting with the parish-level Kirk Sessions, moving upwards to the regional presbytery courts, and then for the most serious cases the General Assembly. Like many early modern justice systems, the accused was considered guilty until proven innocent.

Cases involving fornication or sexual relationships outside marriage were often brought before the church courts, and the accused shamed. Sex outside marriage was a common, if illicit, part of daily life and the fines associated with penance were a significant part of the church's income. The procedure for fornication penance often started when a single woman was seen to be pregnant or after the birth of an illegitimate child. If the child's father did not come forward, then she would be asked to name him so that he could confess and agree to pay child support, avoiding the child becoming a charge on the parish. Some particularly harsh churches were known to interrogate a woman while she was in labour, threatening to withhold the services of a midwife if she would not part with the information.

The confessions of both parents were required for an illegitimate child to be baptised, although a woman could proceed with penance without her professed partner coming forward. Once the confession was made, each paid a fine up to ten pounds – the equivalent of a year's wages for a female servant. Men unable to pay the fine faced imprisonment, whipping or banishment, while women could have their heads shaved, be branded or ducked in the nearest harbour or loch.

Penance for fornication meant spending three humiliating Sundays on the 'stool of repentance' at the front of the Kirk, wearing penitential linen or sackcloth and being referred to in the minister's sermon in full view of the congregation. Women penitents who hid their faces with their plaids were rebuked. Laughing, crying or responding to mockery from the congregation was not allowed. In order to ensure a proper Sunday service, one church reputedly held a Saturday night rehearsal. Some pregnant women denied fornication when accused by the Kirk Session. Knowing that a confession was required to set in motion the expensive and humiliating process of penitence and absolution, they wanted to keep their pride intact a little longer.

By 1690, those in control of the General Assembly of the Church of Scotland set out to narrow further still the path of morality. They believed that the early reformers had been too liberal towards their congregations. Leaders found this new, harsher morality difficult to impose, as the civil courts would no longer support excommunication for minor crimes, such as missing church services and fornication. The civil authorities did, however, introduce An Act Anent [Against] the Murdering of Children in 1690.

Chapter Three

Orray and Idle Women

the impulse of a just horror for the unnatural crime of infanticide, ran the risk of itself occasioning the worst of murders, the death of an innocent person, to atone for a supposed crime which may never have been committed by anyone.

(Sir Walter Scott, *The Heart of Midlothian*, 1818)

The same control, repression, and contempt for women persisted as the late medieval period slid into the early modern period. The Church continued to dominate the everyday lives of Scottish people. The General Assembly had the state at its beck and call, with ministers constantly reminding sheriffs that they could be heavily fined if they did not enforce the law according to the Church's commands. Ordinary men and women were also fined for their misdemeanours, which in an age of drunkenness, cursing, and lax morals were numerous. In 1715, 21 people were prosecuted before the Sheriff of Paisley for 'uncleanliness'. The majority of offenders continued to be women, many convicted for nothing more than 'loose and disorderly' behaviour.

While the state was punishing women according to the code of the church, the church was cultivating a new category of criminals – child murderers. The crime of infanticide was becoming widespread, in part due to the terror women felt at the hated ordeal of being disciplined for immorality before the congregation. Margaret Tait, executed for child murder in 1681, confessed that wishing to avoid being disgraced and ridiculed while being chained to a stake, was the main reason she killed her illegitimate child. On 24 January of the same year, seven more women were executed in Edinburgh for child murder. Research carried out by Deborah A. Symonds for her book *Weep not for Me* (1997) shows that during the years 1691 to 1821 some 347 women were indicted or investigated for infanticide, after attempting to conceal their pregnancy.

The Scottish Parliament was greatly concerned not only by the number of women giving birth in secret, smothering or abandoning their new born children, but also by the expense incurred by town councils in having to support an increasing number of foundlings. As a result of their concern in 1690, new legislation, An Act Anent the Murdering of Children (later known as The Concealment of Pregnancy Act), was passed. A major reason for the introduction of this harsh act was to remove all doubt in the minds of jury members asked to hang a woman who had lost her child. It seems that the 15 good men of the jury often found it difficult to decide whether a child's death was due to natural causes or wilful murder. The 1690 Act was designed to clarify the position of the law and remove any such doubt:

> *If any woman shall conceal her being with child during the whole space, and shall not call or make use of help and assistance in the birth, the child being found dead or missing, the woman shall be holden and repute the murderer of her own child, though there be no appearance or bruise or wound upon the body of the child.*

Such wording left single women between a rock and a hard place when the birth of their child was imminent. To call for the help of a midwife was to bring the child's illegitimacy to the attention of the Kirk. If the child was born alive, but died of exposure after she abandoned it in a public place, then the mother could find herself accused of child murder.

The Concealment of Pregnancy Act, however increased the number of executions. In 1705, four women from Aberdeen were hanged for child murder and in 1714 three more executions took place. In *Twisted Sisters* (2002), Anne Marie Kilday describes three common characteristics that could be attributed to accused women: they were acting alone; they were unmarried; and they were usually employed in domestic service. These characteristics coincide with key factors related to the increase in convictions for infanticide after the Act of 1690. Firstly, the legal statute was unique in Scots Law at that time, in that it presumed the accused party guilty rather than innocent. Secondly, after the crime of assault of authority, child murder was the most frequently indicted offence against the person levelled at women. Finally, child murder was a specifically female crime, usually carried out by women acting alone. Most of the accused women were single, or in the case of Maggie Dickson, women who found themselves alone through no fault of their own.

Maggie Dickson: *Half-Hangit Maggie*

Maggie Dickson was a fish-hawker and a married woman, who bore her fisherman husband several children before he was press-ganged into joining the navy. While her husband was at sea, Maggie took lodgings at a local inn in exchange for work and became pregnant by William Bell, the landlord's son. Should her employer have discovered her pregnancy it would have meant instant dismissal, so Maggie decided to hide her condition for as long as possible. It is not clear whether Maggie gave birth to a live child or a stillborn baby, as she claimed. However, the body of a new born was found near her home and Maggie was escorted to the tolbooth in Edinburgh.

At that time, infection and outbreaks of disease ravaged the tolbooth, which was a multi-storied slum, near St Giles Cathedral. There were no windows, no exercise yard, and the building played host to a large colony of rats. In fact, it conformed to what Scots Law classed '*squalor carcercis*', meaning 'dirty prison'; the principle being that the awfulness of the prison was a necessary part of a felon's punishment.

At Maggie's trial, witnesses came forward to explain that a child had been found near her home. The doctor summoned described how he had submerged the child's lungs in water, where they were found to rise. It was a common belief that if no air had been drawn into the lungs they would sink. The jury pronounced Maggie guilty of child murder and sentenced her to death. On 2 September

1724, she stood on the gallows and admitted to sinning against her husband, but denied the murder of her child. To protect the sensibilities of the masses enjoying the free entertainment, a bag was put over her head before the noose was placed around her neck. She tried to loosen the rope with her hands and John Dalgleish the hangman hit out at her with a stick. The crowd then stoned Dalgleish for not tying her hands tightly enough.

Afterwards, Maggie was pronounced dead. Usually the corpses of those executed were handed over to the medical schools, but in this case her family was allowed to claim the body for burial. Maggie's grieving relatives set off with the coffin on a cart, bound for her home town of Musselburgh. Halfway along the road they stopped outside an inn for refreshment. One member of the party heard a tapping from within the coffin, and when the lid was removed, the corpse sat up. Customers fled the inn, while a doctor bled Maggie and put her to bed.

Having been declared dead, Maggie could not be hanged again for the same offence. The crowd who condemned her on the scaffold now regarded her as a heroine and named her 'Half-hangit Maggie'. She lived for another 29 years, dying of natural causes in 1753.

Isobel Walker: ***Potions, Pills and Good Advice***

Women were once well aware of the high risk of dying in the childbed or of related diseases and almost all would have lost friends and relatives in childbirth. Yet, during the early eighteenth century there was little medical science could do to save them. Married women with access to a doctor's advice and a handful of medical books, perhaps Dr Hugh Chamberlen's translation of *Mauriceau's Traité des Maladies des Femmes Grosses* and homemade potions, were still frightened of giving birth. Those forced to conceal their condition and give birth alone must have been terrified.

Some young women carried their child with no problems at all, but a great number suffered from sickness, headaches, and general discomfort. A wide range of remedies were available to those who could depend upon the support of family and friends. Some remedies, such as blood-letting, were recommended by doctors but mainly suggestions consisted of herbal treatments concocted at home. While a few were effective, most were of little help and formulated according to old spells and superstitions. Anna Hepburn, a member of the Grant Clan is said to have been convinced that wearing a taffeta bag filled with saffron around the neck would prevent a miscarriage. As saffron was a foreign and expensive spice, it can be assumed that she only gave this advice to wealthy women. Other preventative remedies could be equally expensive. One recipe involved mixing ground pearls, gold, and coral with plantain juice.

Perhaps the best advice, requiring no cost, was given by an Edinburgh doctor, William Eccles. The doctor recommended that his patients did not lift heavy items or stretch during the first four months of pregnancy – advice still given today. Eccles was also ahead of his time in suggesting that some physical defect might prevent a woman carrying a foetus to full term. If a child was overdue, the mother was given honey and mint in boiled water to bring on labour. This was only marginally more effective than the 'magic girdle' that Highland women fastened around the mother-to-be in order to speed up contractions.

When women living in large country houses gave birth, a midwife would be summoned before labour started and she would stay with the family until the birth. Although experienced, these professional midwives were not formally trained, instead teachings were passed down through the oral tradition. In 1651 Nicholas Culpepper published his *Directory for Midwives* in Edinburgh. As female literacy was almost non-existent amongst the lower classes, it is doubtful whether many midwives were able to follow Culpepper's instructions.

In poorer homes, an experienced relative or neighbour would assist at the birth. Women who concealed their pregnancies were not afforded this luxury, as the suspicions of a neighbour or local gossip could attract the attention of the authorities. Many unfortunate countrywomen, afraid of the shame and potential punishment, found their way to Edinburgh and sought a secluded spot where they could give birth secretly and anonymously. Once the child was born the mother might leave it on a doorstep or in the wynd where it was born, in the hope that it would be well cared for. She would then return home, nursing her secret.

In 1737 Isobel Walker, the daughter of a farm labourer from the hamlet of Cluden near Dumfries, aroused the suspicions of her neighbours after hiding her pregnancy. She was arrested and imprisoned on a charge of child murder. According to Walter Scott, who heard the tale from a Miss Goldie and a Helen Walker, who claimed to be Isobel's sister, the Walker sisters earned a modest living from spinning, knitting and selling produce from their smallholding. It would have been hard for Isobel to conceal her pregnancy from Helen, the elder of the sisters by several years. Being a religious, god-fearing woman, Helen could not utter a word to help her sister during her trial. Yet, after Isobel was convicted, Helen is said to have walked the 350 miles to London to beg a pardon from King George II.

There is no record of Helen Walker in the surviving High Court records, instead the account suggests that Isobel lived with only her mother. What is certain though, is that Isobel Walker was convicted of child murder and the death sentence pronounced upon her. Few women openly confessed to infanticide in the early eighteenth century and records of trials were poorly kept, but from what remains of the account of Isobel's trial the following information can be gleaned from witness statements. Late in October 1736 just before Hallowmass, William Johnston, a mill owner, was walking along the banks of the Cluden Water when he came upon a dead baby, lying on a sandbank. The new born, male child had been trussed up with one arm tied to his head by an old blue and white handkerchief, which also covered his mouth and nose. He was otherwise naked. The child's body was carried a mile and a half to Nether Cluden parish church.

Later that day, Isobel Walker was confronted by a group of women led by an Emelia Walker (no relation), who physically attacked her. For some time Emelia and other women in the town had suspected that Isobel was carrying a child, though she had continuously denied it. That day Emelia had persuaded a neighbour to send for Isobel. The neighbour warned Isobel of the suspicion she lay under and suggested she allow Emelia and other women to inspect her, as this would vindicate her if she was not pregnant. Isobel responded that she had never been with child and would allow the women to inspect her, but not that day. Emelia arrived with an accomplice, and they grabbed Isobel. She fought and struggled, until a group of women came to the attackers' aid. They ripped her clothes off and found her breasts obviously full of milk. Now that they had the proof they needed, Isobel, still protesting that she had never given birth, was released and allowed to return to her mother's house.

News of the dead child must have reached Emelia Walker quite quickly, as after he had lain a short time at the church, she fetched the child's body from the church and carried it to Isobel's home. With the dead child placed on her knee and surrounded by neighbours, Isobel was examined by a midwife. Afterwards she admitted to having given birth, but claimed that the baby, a girl was born prematurely and that she had thrown her small body into the Cluden Water. Regarding herself as in charge of the situation, Emelia Walker insisted that Isobel had been pregnant since May or June. If the other women realised, as they surely must have, that if Isobel had carried a full-term child she must have conceived in February or March, none said as much.

Isobel was then required to give evidence before the local church minister and Kirk elders. On this occasion she admitted to having given birth five days previously and claimed that her child had been stillborn. She also named David Stott, a tenant farmer as the father. In a statement Stott made the following day, he admitted having 'carnal dealings' with Isobel that February. He explained that he had heard she was 'with child to him', but when he asked her if this was true, she had denied it. John Stott did not testify at Isobel's trial, only those present when she was examined, gave evidence. The most damning evidence came not from Emelia Walker, but from Jean Alexander, a 22-year-old unmarried woman from the village.

Jean claimed not to have suspected that Isobel was pregnant, but informed the court that on the Sunday Isobel gave birth, she had visited Mrs Walker's house. Soon after Jean's arrival, Isobel apparently left her mother and Jean chatting and went off to the back of the house. Shortly afterwards, someone could be heard moaning in the other room. Neither of the women, apparently deep in conversation, had been curious enough to investigate, she told the court.

On 1 May 1738, a jury of 15 male property-owners found Isobel Walker guilty of child murder and the judge sentenced her to be hanged at Dumfries, between three and four o'clock on 14 June. On 12 June, a great seal warrant from George II arrived, postponing her execution for two months. One month later, on 12 July, Isobel was pardoned but banished from 'the Kingdoms of Britain and Ireland'.

The story of Helen Walker's long journey to London to obtain a pardon for her sister has been passed down the generations and fictionalised by Sir Walter Scott in his novel *The Heart of Midlothian* (1818). Did Isobel have a sister whose testimony was omitted from the trial records? If such a sister had existed could she have walked the long miles to London and captured the king's attention in six weeks? The truth of the matter remains a mystery.

Margaret Magnusdaughter: *Three Times A Fornicator*

Although a murdering mother was regarded as an unnatural monster in the seventeenth and eighteenth centuries, she was, in most cases, a victim of circumstance, rather than the perpetrator of an evil act. Many women hid their pregnancy to avoid the shame of being dragged before the Kirk Sessions.

In November 1698, Margaret Magnusdaughter, a servant from the Tingwall parish of Shetland, was summoned before the Kirk

Session to answer a rumour that she was with child. Although she denied it, the Kirk elders ignored her protest of innocence, believing Margaret to be a 'baise and vyld strumpet'. She had appeared before the session accused of fornication on three previous occasions, and was branded a 'trelaps fornicatrix' (three-times fornicator) by the local community (Lyn Abrams, *Twisted Sisters*).

The following January, Margaret appeared once more before the Kirk Sessions. On this occasion she first admitted to having been pregnant and claimed the father of the child was a strange man who had lodged in her master's house and had now left. Yet, she later said that her employer, Erasmus Irvine was the true father and she had not told anyone of her condition, nor called for assistance during the birth. She had aborted the child on her own and Irvine had taken the body away. It is not known whether this information was given up voluntarily, or extracted under torture, for it was not uncommon for church elders to use violent means to extract a confession. As a result, however, Margaret appeared at the local sheriff court on 17 January 1699, charged with murdering her new born child.

Most women were accused of having acted alone but Margaret's case was unusual in that she appeared with three co-defendants. Barbara Marwick from Orkney and John Mowat had allegedly supplied Margaret with a drink to bring about an abortion. Erasmus Irvine, who had broken down before the Kirk Session and admitted being the child's father and disposing of its body, was charged with 'concealing and conniving of in … the murder of the child'. Under the Concealment of Pregnancy Act, all four defendants could be sentenced to death for committing, 'so horrabill and detestable a crime a[s] murthering ane poor innocent infant, a lyf in the mother's belly not come to the light of the world'.

It could be argued from the evidence given at the trial that Margaret acted under the influence of Erasmus Irvine. He was desperate to be rid of an illegitimate child and it was Irvine who had gone to great trouble and expense to procure an abortifacient when Margaret was five weeks into her pregnancy. There was no one though, who felt sympathetic enough to argue this point for a woman who constantly defied the Kirk Session and was judged to lead an immoral life. Despite the cause of the child's death being unclear throughout the trial, Justice William Menzies convicted Margaret Magnusdaughter, Erasmus Irvine and Barbara Marwick of child murder. The evidence against Mowat was judged to be insufficient.

A woman's age, her experience, and as in the case of Margaret Magnusdaughter, her reputation, all influenced the way in which her physical symptoms were interpreted by the community and the courts. Pregnancy was not easily diagnosed until the twentieth century and a woman could take advantage of the uncertainty surrounding a diagnosis when denying her condition. Many women though, did not deliberately conceal their pregnancies but were without knowledge of the signs and symptoms. Ignorance however, was not a defence accepted by either the Kirk Session or the courts. To ensure a jury could not be swayed by the defendant pleading ignorance of the Act, it was publicly displayed throughout Scotland and read out regularly in the churches.

Common Adulterous Whores

It was not only the morality of pregnant and unmarried women that was closely monitored; all single women came under scrutiny. The local Kirk maintained a strong influence over all individuals in the community, but the vast majority of women offenders brought before the courts were accused of similar, specifically female, crimes, such as being 'a common adulterous whore' and the lesser charge of 'bad behaviour and very unseemly carriage'.

Within the Kirk walls women were treated differently to men and required to sit separately. In the days when sermons were three or four hours long, women often took a well-earned nap. In May 1604, Glasgow Kirk Session ordered that no woman could wear her plaid around her head in church, as many used this disguise to conceal the fact they were asleep throughout the sermon. A beadle carrying a white stick was appointed to wake slumbering women and offenders were required to appear at the pillar for 'troubling' the Kirk.

Just as there were certain charges reserved solely for women, so women were allocated their own occupations. Midwifery was perceived as an acceptable vocation, as women learned to deliver children from their own experience. In the countryside, women worked the land alongside their men, while townswomen kept lodging houses or modest inns, and some were run on a much grander scale. A 1771 edition of the *Glasgow Journal* advertised the White Hart Inn in Gallowgate, managed by a Mrs Parlance.

In Glasgow, 'keeping a mangle' was a lucrative business. On Glasgow Green, the town's common washing area, an army of women trampling clothes and bed linen in boynes, or tubs, was a common sight. Many a male voyeur is said to have sneaked on to the green for a closer look at the women with their skirts rolled up around their thighs. He took his pleasure at his own peril, for, if caught, the washerwomen would attack him with any makeshift weapons to hand. To preserve the women's modesty, the Glasgow Green wash-house was built in 1732 and later extended to accommodate 200 washerwomen.

Almost all occupations taken up by women complied with the traditional image of a woman's role in society. Although the Scottish theatre had recovered from the draconian measures imposed by the Reformation, it was still not open to Scots-born actresses. It would seem, though, that foreign women were allowed to perform in Edinburgh as early as the seventeenth century. Outside the theatre, acrobatic acts were quite common on the city streets. Juggling, vaulting and tightrope walking all formed part of street entertainment performed on temporary stages, some devised by quack doctors to promote their medicines. In the 1660s and 1670s, unusually one performer was a woman, a tumbler called Joanna Baptista Quarentina.

Independent single or 'orray' women earning their own living were sometimes considered to be out of control. Glasgow Town

Council forbade single women, as well as vagabonds and beggars of either sex, from living alone or renting property together. The Kirk's obsession for social control did not end with heterosexual parishioners. If discovered, same sex couples could be accused of the 'slaunderous behaviour of sodomy' and forbidden each other's company.

For much of Scotland's past, women had little or no autonomy over their own lives and those brave enough to defy the Kirk, often found themselves at the end of the hangman's rope.

Chapter Four

Ladies of the Land

They said, I had neither cow nor calf,
Nor dribbles o' drink rins throw the draff …
(Lady Grisell Baillie, 'The Ladies of the Covenant')

At the close of the seventeenth century around 90 per cent of Scotland's population of one million dwelt on the land and relied on the productivity of its farms for their living. Since the early years of the century, people were divided into social classes determined by their economic position in the farming community. At the top of the social ladder were the tenant farmers, who rented directly from the landowner.

The tenant farmers believed themselves to be the aristocracy of the farming community and many claimed the empty title of 'gentleman'. The tenant farmers might have thought themselves gentlemen, but their wives certainly did not lead the lives of ladies. Agriculture relied heavily on female labour and it was the job of the farmer's wife to help with the harvest, cut the hay, bring in the peats, tend the limekiln, cart and carry the stacks for threshing and all before mucking out the byre.

On the next tier of this social structure were the sub-tenant farmers, who would in turn give 'cotters' or labourers, a piece of land to work. Some areas limited the number of cotters according to the size of the farm. These restrictions meant an increase in the number of unmarried and landless males having to move to another area to find work.

Women living on the coast worked just as hard as their farming equivalents. On the days when their husbands decided to go to sea (that is, when a pig did not cross his path, a church minister was not seen near the boat, and neither these nor one of a hundred other 'unlucky' events did not prevent him from sailing), fishwives would start the day by carrying their men out to the boats. Before harbours were built in many small coastal villages, the women carried the men on their backs to prevent the woollen socks they had so carefully knitted getting wet. When fishwives were not mending or baiting nets, seeing to the children, housework and other chores, they were knitting. A woman who did not have her hands full every minute of the day was considered lazy and sluttish by her neighbours.

Some women in the North East of Scotland were able to bring in a little cash by spinning and working extra stockings and plaids to sell to Aberdeen merchants. Highland chiefs and peasants alike wore the plaid, a long woollen blanket that served as a cloak by day and a coverlet by night. The more affluent could afford thin shoes, bonnet, doublet and stockings. Most men however just wore a waistcoat and knee length shirt belted round the middle to hide their lack of underwear. Women wore a plaid draped over their heads and pinned over their bosoms, and a linen skirt. Peasant women did not wear shoes, except to church.

No amount of women's labour though, could raise a family out of the terrible poverty that existed throughout the country. In remote regions there was no trade or market for the fishwives to take their catch and barter for clothes or oats and barley. No recognisable road system existed in the early eighteenth century, only a network of rough tracks suitable for sturdy ponies or moving cattle but mostly impassable to four wheel carts. Labourers on every rung of the social ladder were poverty-stricken and oppressed for several reasons, chiefly the tyranny of custom and superstition.

Open, treeless landscapes, with great expanses of wasteland, left the crops exposed to the elements and hungry, marauding cattle. Landlords in the first quarter of the eighteenth century, wishing to enclose their lands by building dykes or planting hedges, met fierce opposition. In Galloway large bands of women and men armed with pitchforks and stakes overturned dykes and spoiled hedges in nightly raids.

Land was considered cultivated if it produced two seeds for one sown, and four seeds was regarded a good crop. On the farms, the grain sown by farmers was the poorest sort, grey oats, which at its best only gave three seeds to one. Bere, the least nutritious of all barley was grown for making ale. These were the only two crops sown and the ground was cultivated until it produced only two seeds for every one sown and every third year produced a 'wersh crop', miserable in quality and quantity. Farmers stuck to their ancient system, placing their faith in the old sayings:

If land be three years out and three years in,
T'will keep in good heart ti the deil grow blin.

At times, however, old beliefs and religious feelings gave way to idleness and hampered agriculture. Long drawn-out holy days and fairs encouraged women and men to desert their fields at the most crucial times of the year, leaving the crops at the mercy of ill weather. Also, new and innovative ideas were resisted. Until the 1740s, barley was ground by bruising it in a mortar or 'knocking stones' and adding a little water to make the grain part with the husk. Yet, over 30 years earlier, Andrew Fletcher of Saltoun in East Lothian discovered a new milling process in Holland and ordered his wheelwright to make up the machines. The mill together with an adjoining enterprise for making Holland cloth was run by his sister-in-law. 'Saltoun Barley Meal' was a great success and was stocked by retailers all over the country. Other barley producers stubbornly held on to the old crude and wasteful method.

The old feudal system of paying rents and wages in kind contributed to both the workers' poverty and the landowners' lack of silver. Only unskilled farm labourers and women were paid in cash. The superior farmworkers, such as ploughmen and threshers, received a cottage with its own kail-yard and some ground for growing oats and bere instead of cash wages. Rents were likewise paid in kind. Landlords held barns full of livestock, meal, malt, poultry, pigeons, beans and other commodities paid by their tenants. This often meant that landlords, too, were short of cash but many were still able to indulge in the vice of gluttony. Landlords' lifestyles varied according to the size of their lands. One landowner, Sir Rory Mor Macleod, was infamous for his uproarious hospitality at Dunvegan Castle. In the 1580s the chief was receiving 9,000 hens a year and 400 stones of butter from the Isle of Skye alone and added to this there was a great store of mutton, venison, and game. Wine, sugar and spices could be imported from France in exchange for salmon or other produce from the estate.

Wives, no matter how wealthy, kept a close eye on their larder and the household budget. Ladies kept rings to measure the size of eggs. The lady of the house also chose the food for the table. The Duchess of Buccleuch and Monmouth made sure that each guest did not eat a menu above his station, whilst entertaining the Earls of Rothes and Haddington at Dalkeith.

Dinner Menu, Saturday 8 November 1701

Her Grace's Table (family and six guests)

First Course

200 Oysters

Bacon and pease pottage

Haggis with a calf's pluck

Beef collops

Mutton roast, three joints

Fricassee of five chickens

Roasted Goose

Second Course

Six wild fowl and six chickens

Buttered crabs

Collard beef

Tarts

Four roasted hens

Stewards' Table

Beef, one piece

Roasted mutton, two joints

Officers' Table

Beef, two pieces

Roasted mutton, two joints

Last Table

Roasted mutton, eight joints.

(Arnot, *History of Edinburgh*, 1780)

The hangers-on at the last table may have felt like the poor relations, but it was an improvement on the average diet of the Duchess's tenants. The typical daily intake of farmers and labourers on the east of Scotland during the seventeenth century consisted of:

Breakfast

Oatmeal porridge with milk or ale

Or

Broth made of cabbage left overnight and oat bannock

Dinner

Sowans (a type of porridge) with oatcake and kail

Supper

Kail with oatcakes.

After the Restoration, among the upper classes lavish household consumption was reduced, although it is obvious from Lady Buccleuch's menu that the noble classes still ate prodigious amounts of meat and few vegetables. With more landowners turning towards livestock, such as black cattle, which could be traded for silver, their inclination now was towards acquiring cutlery, linen and napery (table linen) rather than giving way to intermittent bouts of gluttony.

A few titled ladies not only kept control of the household larder, but became the driving force behind successful and financially profitable businesses, like Anne, the 3rd Duchess of Hamilton (1631–1716). The daughter of Lady Mary Feilding, one of Queen Henrietta Maria's ladies of the bedchamber, Anne rebuilt the local burgh school, provided new alms houses, and established a wool factory and a spinning school from the proceeds of her Hamilton estates. Anne also introduced coal-mining, a salt pan and a ferry boat on her island of Arran, earning her the title of the 'Good Duchess Anne' amongst the people of western Scotland.

On the outbreak of the English Civil War, Anne was sent from Chelsea by her father James, 1st Duke of Hamilton, to be brought up by her grandmother on the family estates. When her father was executed by the Cromwellians, Anne's uncle inherited his lands, then when the second Duke was fatally wounded at the Battle of Worcester, they passed to Anne. Although in theory she had become Scotland's greatest heiress, aged just 19, she was forced to take a small house near Hamilton Palace for all her estates had been confiscated by Cromwell due to her father and uncle's involvement in the Civil War. They were later restored by the Protectorate in 1657.

Anne married the Catholic William Douglas, Earl of Selkirk in 1656, even though her father had stipulated that she was to marry a Protestant. It seems to have been both a love match and a companionable marriage. Gradually the couple managed to pay all the outstanding fines, allowing them to reclaim the estate. They developed the plans for the expansion that Anne carried out after his death, as well as laying out extensive gardens at Hamilton Palace.

In sharp contrast, the wife of the average husbandman could boast neither cultivated gardens nor any luxuries for the dining table in her home. Most agricultural labourers lived in a space divided up to contain family and livestock, as well as servants if they were prosperous. The farm worker and his family had little furniture. A boxbed for the head of the family and his wife, straw mattresses for the family and servants, a meal kist, a few stools, cups, bowls, spoons and cooking pots were likely to make up the family's household effects. Most houses consisted of stone walls without mortar and a wooden ridge top roof, covered with lumps of turf, which were held together by heather thatching. A small vent in the roof acted as an escape for smoke from the central fire. There were no windows or doors, only an opening in the wall. Privvies, or toilets, comprising three seats were built outside, adjacent to the house. Excrement fell into an open midden yard, where it piled up until cleared away to be spread upon the land. Both the outside and interior of many houses were filthy. It was a state the inhabitants revelled in, for it saved them the trouble of cleaning and the dirt kept them warm. Among popular contemporary sayings were, 'The clartier the cosier' and 'Muck makes luck'.

Architectural designs varied depending on the amount of timber available. In a countryside largely devoid of trees, the wooden beams forming the roof were the most valuable part of the dwelling. If the tenant was forced to move, then it was quite common for him to take the roof with him. Baronial courts took a dim view of such outright theft.

The Baronial Court had a dual purpose: as a place where tenants met to interpret custom and also as the laird's private court of jurisdiction, where he could exert his control over his tenants and punish crimes committed against himself or the community. These courts were much concerned with social order and the behaviour of women. It was common in some areas for wives to be banned from drinking alcohol unless their husbands were present.

Grisell Hume, Lady Baillie: *An Undercover Agent and Writer of Ballads*

Illiteracy was the rule rather than the exception amongst the farming communities, with a smaller percentage of literate women than men. Yet, in recording their lives, the educated noblewoman and the illiterate tenant's wife had one thing in common – the ballad.

Grisell Hume, Lady Baillie of Jerviswood, was born on 25 December 1665, the eldest of Sir Patrick Hume, Baron of Polwarth and Grisell Kerr's 18 children. She began her life in troubled times. In 1675, under the Administration of the Duke of Lauderdale, the Privy Council ordered garrisons to be stationed in the houses of certain noblemen and gentlemen to deter Covenanters from holding conventicles (outdoor prayer meetings). The soldiers were to be supplied with meal, pots, pans and candles at the owner's expense. Patrick Hume complained to the council that such an imposition was illegal and appealed to the Court of Session for compensation. With the approval of Charles II, Hume was imprisoned for 'being a fractious person'.

After her father's release from gaol, when she was around ten or eleven years old, her parents began sending Grisell on confidential missions. On one such errand Grisell was sent to visit her father's friend Robert Baillie, who was in prison for rescuing his brother-in-law from a persecutor. Her parents believed that as a child she would find it easier to gain access to his cell. After a long walk to Edinburgh from her country home, Grisell did indeed see Baillie and slip him a letter containing vital information and advice. On this visit Grisell first saw Mr Baillie's son George, who was to be her future husband.

After her successful visit to Robert Baillie, Grisell was sent on many such adventures and when, in 1679, her father was imprisoned once more, this time in Edinburgh Tolbooth and Dumbarton Castle, again she smuggled in letters containing important intelligence. Yet, in 1683, Patrick Hume was accused of taking part in a conspiracy to prevent a Catholic succession to the British throne and he felt it necessary to hide in the family vault at Polwarth Church, a mile from his home. He stayed concealed in the graveyard for a month, during which time Grisell visited him at midnight, bringing him food and drink, despite her fear of the dead.

There was some difficulty in obtaining food for him without arousing the servants' suspicions and from Grisell's biography, written by her eldest daughter Grisell, Lady Murray of Stanhope, we learn that she stole the food from the dinner table and dropped it onto her lap. Apparently Grisell's father was very fond of sheep's head and one day, whilst her brothers and sisters supped their broth, she concealed the sheep's head on her lap. Her nine-year-old brother Alexander, still hungry, looked towards the empty plate and exclaimed "Mother, will you look at Grisell; while we have been eating our broth, she has eat up the whole sheep's head".

As the vault was not fit for habitation, Grisell and her mother formed a plan to hide Patrick Hume under a bed in their home. With the help of a trusted servant, James Winter, Grisell dug out a hole in the ground underneath the bed with her bare hands. Any noise from using tools might have attracted unwanted attention. Winter then constructed a coffin-like box with air holes and Grisell lined it with bed linen. After a few weeks, the box began to fill with water and Hume decided it was time to leave his family and escape to Holland. This decision coincided with the news that his old friend Robert Baillie had been executed at the cross of Edinburgh.

After his escape to Holland, Hume was formally charged with 'contriving the death of his majesty and his brother The Duke of York, overturning the government, converse with rebels and the concealing of treason'. As a traitor his estates, goods and rents were forfeited to the Crown. Now almost destitute, Grisell and her family set sail for Rotterdam to join Hume in Utrecht. They would later return with William, Prince of Orange, and his fleet when he invaded England in protest of James VII's intention to re-establish Catholicism in England.

During her three and a half year exile in Holland Grisell wrote poetry. Part of one such ballad, shows her skill for composition:

When bonny young Johnny came o'er the sea,
He said he saw naething sae lovely as me;
He hecht me baith rings and mony braw things;
And were na my heart licht I wad dee

He had a wee titty that loo'ed na me,
Because I was twice as bonny as she;
She rais'd such a pother 'twixt him and his mother,
That were na my heart licht I wad dee.

The day it was set, and the bridal to be,
The wife took a dwam, and lay down to dee,

She main'd and she grain'd out o' dolour and pain,
Till he vow'd he never wad see me again,

His kin was for ane o' a higher degree,
Said, what had he to do with the like of me?
Albeit I was bonny, I was na for Johnny:
And were no my heart licht I wad die,

They said, I had neither cow nor calf,
Nor dribbles o' drink rins throw the draff,
Nor pickles o' meal rins throw the mill-ee:
And were na my heart licht I wad dee.

('The Ladies of the Covenant')

In real life Grisell was married to George Baillie for around 46 years and according to Grisell's wishes she was buried next to George in a monument at Mellerstain. Her funeral took place on her birthday, Christmas day 1746. However, Grisell's lyrics demonstrate, alongside her mastery of the formulaic structures of the courtship ballad, that there are only two results of courtship in the ballad world: marriage or death.

The cantadora (keeper of the old stories) and Jungian psychoanalyst Clarissa Pinkola Estes points out in her book *Women Who Run With the Wolves*, that the stories of ballad heroines cannot be studied, they are 'learned through assimilation, through living in its proximity with those who know it, live it and teach it – more so through all the day to day mundane tasks of life'. In ballads composed by literate women like Grisell, the Scottish heroine is different in one vital way to those depicted in traditional stories, ballads and fairy tales from other nations; she does not rely on a man to rescue her from her predicament but uses her own resources. In cases where courtship leads her to the gallows, she chooses her own fate and if that should be death, then she will stand alone and in her gallows speech address the crowd articulately and eloquently.

In the following example from one of the many versions of the popular infanticide ballad 'Mary Hamilton', the character of Mary, who attends Mary Queen of Scots, is wronged by Henry Stuart, Lord Darnley. She drowns the child he fathered by her and makes it perfectly clear that she does not want 'the highest Stuart of all' to rescue her. When Darnley appears and tells her to get down from the gallows 'for tonight you will dine with me' she replies:

Aw hold your tongue my sovereign liege
And let your folly be
For if you'd a mind to save my life
You'd never have shamed me here
Last night there were four Marys
Tonight they'll be but three
There was Mary Beaton, Mary Seaton
And Mary Carmichael and me.

Of course many educated women led privileged lives and did not experience the same courtship rituals as their less fortunate sisters; women who did not have the education, confidence or courage to make a grand speech from the scaffold. Nor did many literate women find themselves in the unfortunate position of Mary Stuart's legendary maid. They learned of the average woman's often tragic courtship from their servants. Maids would relate tales from the 'Rockings', moonlight meetings in barns or cottages. Young women brought along their rocks and reels or distaffs and spindles, and sat spinning wool and flax whilst the young men courted them, for all courtships evolved around work. There was much song and merriment.

Many fine ballads were composed and passed down by the oral tradition, but a great many of the songs sung at such gatherings, like 'Wooing the Maiden' and 'Waste and Thrift', were earthy and told of bargaining over tochers and uncouth wooing with sly innuendoes and coarse speech.

Chapter Five

Such a Parcel of Rogues

Oh would, ere I had seen the day
That treason thus could sell us,
My auld grey heid had lien in clay
Wi Bruce and loyal Wallace
But Pith and Power, till my last hour,
I'll mak this declaration;
We're bought and sold for English gold-
Such a parcel of rogues in a nation!

(Robert Burns, 'Such a Parcel of Rogues in a Nation', 1791)

At the turn of the eighteenth century, Edinburgh was a capital city split by the extreme differences in the quality of life expected by the nobility, the middle classes and the poor. The landed gentry lived in fortified grandeur outside the city and settled their disputes with 'tulzies' or gentlemanly brawls in the city streets. Merchants and tradesmen took the best ground-floor accommodation and those with little money were pushed further and further skywards in crammed tenement buildings.

The 'crag and tail' topography of the old town was created during the Ice Age, when receding glaciers pushed soft soil aside and the land was split by crags of hard volcanic rock. The hilltop crag was first to be inhabited and fortified, eventually developing into Edinburgh Castle. The rest of the city grew down the tail of land from the castle rock. Due to the narrowness of this 'tail', Edinburgh boasted the earliest high-rise residential buildings. Its tenements had extra floors, added from as early as the 1500s, and poorer residents occupied the smallest rooms, usually in the attics of buildings rising to 10 or 12 storeys. Despite the cramped living conditions nobody wanted to leave the safety of the city and the protection offered by the Flodden Wall. Built in the sixteenth century as a defence against English invaders after James IV's defeat at Flodden Field, the wall offered the type of fortification only available to the powerful and affluent in other parts of the country.

This was the legacy James IV left to Edinburgh, just as his father had added his own defences to the city by way of the Nor' Loch. The Nor' Loch bordered Edinburgh on its north side, where Princes Street Gardens are situated today. In 1460, James III ordered that this forested valley should be dammed and flooded with the natural spring waters. Although intended to strengthen the castle's defences, the Nor' Loch was initially a haven where residents could relax, with boating in the summer and skating in the winter. But by the early 1700s, it was a stinking cesspool full of waste and human excrement. Methane gas from the loch leaked into the closes of the old town and caused hallucinations among the 80,000 residents who were crammed into its narrow streets.

In spite of, or perhaps because of the Nor Loch's toxic emissions, the cesspool held a great attraction for would-be suicides. In *Old and New Edinburgh* (*Vol III*) James Grant describes two failed suicides. A crowd rushed down to the waterside when a man waded into the 'Nor' Loch with the intention of ending his life. Nobody rushed in to save him, but the commotion did wake a Lord in James' Court and cause him to throw up his window and shout down the brae to the people, "What's all the noise about? Can't ye e'en let the man gang to the de'il his ain gate?". Apparently, the man in the water then changed his mind about going to meet his maker and walked out of the loch, to the amusement of the crowd. Later a lady who tried to take her own life was defeated in her attempt, when the hoops of her petticoat kept her afloat.

Generally speaking, the inhabitants of Edinburgh lived quite happily together. The privileged and the penniless walked the filthy streets side by side. In contrast to the squalor, deprivation and mean living conditions that women of the lower social orders were forced to endure, the wealthiest ladies paraded through the High Street and Canongate dressed in their hoops, brocade dresses and brightly-coloured plaids. In these busy thoroughfares, sedan chairs carried by highland porters whisked members of high society off towards the wynds, which were too narrow for horse and carriage. Nobles and caddies, judges and beggars all rubbed shoulders as they went about their business.

Up until around 1745 the hour for dining was one o'clock, when merchants and lawyers would partake of solan goose, cock-a-leekie soup, sheep's head, and haggis before returning to their businesses or the law-courts. The food was usually accompanied by wine and enjoyed in the town's many inns, such as Douglas's Tavern in Anchor Close. Men ate whilst women served them, yet many taverns were run by formidable female publicans, who brewed their own beer. Managing a drinking establishment was considered a suitable profession for a woman as it could be fitted in around housework, cooking and the rearing of children.

Among the higher ranks all over Scotland ladies enjoyed their afternoon reflection at four o'clock. Women in gigantic hoops, carrying huge green paper fans and little bags of snuff, tripped down the filthy streets in three-inch heels to the houses of their hostesses. In larger houses the hostess received her guests in the drawing room, whilst occupants of small flats were obliged to entertain visitors in the bedroom. Until the 1720s, when tea became a popular refreshment, ladies drank copious amounts of ale and claret for several hours, until their maids arrived to light the way home for their mistresses.

Eight o'clock was the supper hour and wealthy citizens ate and drank into the small hours of the morning when guests departed, staggering their way home. The less affluent made do with the penny ale and raw spirits sold in less salubrious establishments and often had to ignore the dinner hour altogether. However, this was a convivial age and a hard-drinking society. The nobility whiled away their evenings singing blasphemous songs in gentlemen's clubs, among them the Sulphur Club, The Hell-Fire Club, and The Horn Club – all condemned by the Kirk for apparently hosting hideous orgies. Professional men met in either Paxton's gloomy inn or the 'coffin', a dingy room in John Dowie's tavern to 'splice the rope', a term used for the entertainment to be had in discussing details of the next day's hanging.

In the company of high-spirited gentlemen, ladies of dubious virtue frequented the dirty, squalid basement rooms that were the oyster bars. Here their raucous laughter and the clatter of their high heels echoed off the cellar walls, as they slurped raw oysters, drank ale and danced the evening away. All entertainment came to an abrupt end when the town guard beat the ten o'clock drum, a warning to all decent burghers to withdraw soberly to bed. As the guard beat his tattoo up and down the High Street and Canongate, the taverns, inns and cellars disgorged their singing patrons out on to the streets in their varying stages of inebriety. Under civic law all citizens were prohibited from being in taverns, inns and change houses (gambling dens) after the beating of the drum. Night-time revelry was seen to be the cause of abounding drunkenness, uncleanliness and a great hindrance to sober persons in the worship of God. Penalties for disobedience were at the discretion of the magistrates and very much depended on how drunk the accused was found to be.

Ten o'clock was a dangerous hour to be wandering the streets in a drunken state, as it was the hour appointed for household waste to be thrown from the tenement windows into the gutters below. Many passers-by who failed to hear the warning shout of "gardy loo" (Gardez a l'eau) or answer "haud yer hand" in time had the malodorous contents of stoups, pots and cans poured upon them as they loitered in the dark wynds. These unfortunate revellers often woke to find themselves covered in the sweet, sickly stench of human excrement known as 'the flowers of Edinburgh'. On rising the hungover residents would burn brown paper to deodorise the airless rooms of overcrowded tenements, whilst out in the streets well-fed pigs poked their snouts amongst the rubbish and grunted in satisfaction.

Sunday Wife Beatings –a Scandalous Crime

With Edinburgh's citizens consuming such a large amount of alcohol, it is hardly surprising that there was a high incidence of domestic violence in the town. It was quite acceptable at the time for men to beat their servants, children and wives. Wife beatings only came to the attention of the Kirk Sessions if the wife was incapacitated on a Sunday or if the uproar caused a public scandal.

In *Sin in the City* (1998), Leah Leneman and Rosalind Mitchison bring to light the cases of John Lauder, who appeared before Leith Kirk Session in February 1704 and William Steven, brought before the St Cuthbert's Kirk Session in July 1712. Lauder confessed that when he had been in drink he had beaten his wife and called her a damned bitch. He claimed that she had provoked him, but that it was the first time he had done it and hoped it would be the last. He was admonished and rebuked with certification that if he was seen drunk again or found to beat his wife he would be rebuked before the congregation and referred to the magistrates.

A thatcher by occupation, William Steven appeared before the Kirk Session eight years later, and was found guilty of 'habitual drunkenness, particularly upon Saturday last the 26th instant he was beastly drunk and did curse, swear and barbarously strike his wife'. When he appeared in court two weeks later he was again drunk and the magistrates ordered him to be locked up so the following day he might be sober enough to understand his punishment. When Steven appeared in court sober the next morning, he expressed a 'sense of sorrow' for his behaviour and 'promised through God's Strength to guard against that beastly Sin'. He was dismissed with the usual rebuke and threat of public appearances if he was found guilty again.

Not all entertainment in Edinburgh revolved around alcohol, although pleasures were somewhat limited by restrictions imposed by the Kirk. Despite the Presbytery's insistence that people refrain from any activity other than attending services on the Sabbath, many enjoyed a Sunday stroll. Idly walking or 'vaiging' in the fields outside the city boundaries was widely condemned from the pulpit, but the activity was so popular it was impossible to single out individuals. At the beginning of the eighteenth century theatre was still seen as the Devil's advocate and performances were severely restricted by religious opposition. Drama consisted of only a few irregular performances at the Tennis Court Theatre at Holyrood. Those who wished to pursue a career in the theatre were forced to move south of the border and either pick up work with provincial companies or continue on to London.

One playwright though, was born in London to a Scottish family and moved north of the border after several well received plays. Catherine Trotter, known as Mrs Cockburn (1679–1749) is said to have written her first published play, *Agnes de Castro*, a reworking of Aphra Behn's own adaptation of a French novel, when she was only 17. Several more plays followed including *Fatal Friendship, Love at a Loss*, and *The Revolution in Sweden*, and were performed to great acclaim. Her second, *Fatal Friendship,* is still recognised as being one of the greatest Restoration plays by a female playwright, but she is probably best known for her works on moral philosophy such as 'A Defence of Mr Locke's Essay of Human Understanding', a response to Locke's theories. Catherine continued with her philosophical works after marrying. She also tried her hand at prose fiction and anonymously published an epistolary novel *Olinda's Adventures; or the Amours of a Young Lady*, in 1693.

For women who were literate, reading matter was hard to come by throughout Scotland. Legislation forbade the publishing of books without the prior consent of the Chancellor, and newspaper articles needed a licence from the Bishop of Edinburgh. At the time no newspapers were being printed on a regular basis. Scotland's first newspaper the *Mercurius Caledonius*, appeared only briefly in 1660 and 1661. Fifteen years later, little was being published except for a few pamphlets, works on law, politics, controversy and badly printed editions of devotional works.

Assessing the poor and limited market, one woman with her eye on the main chance was quick to exploit the situation. The widow of the king's master printer, Mrs Agnes Anderson ensured that she inherited her husband's patent and set herself up in business printing folios of Poole's *Annotations* and Flavel's works – the great authorities of ministers – as well as Bibles, catechisms, and school books. However, her Bibles were full of blasphemous blunders, spelling errors and words that ran into each other. *The Memorial of Bible Societies in Scotland 1824* gives an example: 'whyshoulditbethoug tathing-incredible wtyou, yt God should raise the dead &adamselcamenuntohim'. Mrs Anderson may not have possessed professional printing skills, but she did have a talent for litigation. Her patent gave her works a monopoly and she regularly sued printers in Edinburgh, Glasgow and Aberdeen, until the courts could no longer suffer her law suits or find in her favour against publishers and printers who were creating work of far greater quality.

Among the first newspapers printed in the capital were the *Edinburgh Courant* (later the *Edinburgh Evening Courant*), published 1705 to 1871, and *The Caledonian Mercury*, published three times a week from 1720 to 1867. These were two of the most enduring Scottish newspapers, although circulation in the eighteenth century was very low. Chapbooks, meaning 'cheap' books, were a popular form of street literature. These poorly printed texts had quite a broad content, from sermons of covenanting ministers to prophecies, the last words of murderers and songs. More working people were now becoming literate, including some women. Those who could afford it were able to enjoy Allan Ramsay's circulating library, which loaned out copies of 'profane' books brought from London. Discontented with pious works, literate Scots now enjoyed ungodly plays, poems and scurrilous pamphlets. The lending library opening in the Luckenbooths in 1728 was the first of its kind in the British Isles.

Yet, by far the most popular form of street literature for nearly 300 years was the broadsides, the forerunners of the modern tabloid. Often pinned to the walls of houses and inns, these single sheets informed the public of court proceedings, and executions.

Stories were reported with great immediacy, as competition was fierce and breaking news increased sales. The words were read out for the benefit of those who could not read and provided great entertainment for the ghoulish and the gullible.

Broadsides also provided popular songs of a less refined nature. Two verses taken from a ballad 'The Coalier Lassie' (published c.1701) tells of how the narrator tried to coerce a collier's daughter into losing her virginity to him:

Although at first she may deny,
Yet you must pursue her
Her modesty will make her cry
Your Rudeness will undo her
But with a forward brisk address
Unto the point intended;
First you must Kiss and then Caress,
And so the matter's ended

This was the method that I us'd
While she was denying
And aye the more that she refus'd
The more I was applying
Till the Key of her Virginity
To me she did deliver;
Tho' I like not the Affinity
To receive it was clever.

In the last verse it is revealed that the narrator did not take her virginity, for the Laird, her father's employer had used the same tactics before him.

'The Coalier's Lassie' reveals much about women and class in the early eighteenth century and such information only survives because of the broadsides. Early ballads were dramatic and humorous narrative songs derived from a folk culture that pre-dated printing. Musical notation was rarely published, as tunes were usually established favourites, passed down in the oral tradition. Women in the early 1700s were not only the subject of ballads, but also composed some of Scotland's most enduring and well-known songs. Few though, would admit to having put pen to paper, as composing music was regarded by society as being crude for a woman, perhaps because of the more sexually-explicit ballads appearing at the time.

Drunken Wife Going Cheap

A century later broadsides were no less sensational, as the following account printed in 1828 by a Newcastle publisher demonstrates. Entitled 'Sale of a Wife,' the broadside was advertised as:

> *A full and particular Account of the Sale of a Woman, named Mary Mackintosh, which took place on Wednesday evening the 16th of July, 1828, in the Grass Market of Edinburgh, accused by her husband of being a notorious drunkard; with the particulars of the bloody Battle which took place, afterwards.*

That Wednesday evening, Mary Mackintosh had been brought down to the Grassmarket by her husband, who intended to put her up for sale by auction. She was held by a straw rope around her middle and a notice stating 'To be sold by public auction' was pinned to her bosom. Several thousand spectators turned out and the auctioneer commenced business, but so great was the uproar amongst the crowd, it was ten minutes before he could take an offer. Mary attracted several bids from a Highlander, a tinker and a drunken brogue-maker staggering out of the nearest tavern.

Several hundred local women then moved through the crowd, some throwing stones and others wielding boulders wrapped in stockings, attacking the mob, and knocking down everyone in their way. When they reached the auctioneer, they scratched his face for so insulting a woman. Such was the intensity of the battle that ensued someone might have been killed had it not been for the timely intervention of the police. After the disturbance calmed down, Mary's husband again insisted she should be sold. The auctioneer refused to continue unless he received protection. Several young men in the crowd offered to stand guard and once again Mary was put up for sale. The bidding resumed with an old pensioner leering "she's a tight little frigate and well rigged too", and offering half a crown more than the last bidder. It was to a sympathetic farmer though, that she was finally sold for two pounds and five shillings. He hefted her up on his horse and the pair rode out of the Grassmarket to great cheers from the crowd.

The Darien Disaster

Such public scandals, as well as dark and salacious deeds, ensured maximum sales of these cheap news-sheets and during the years 1699–1707, the failure of the Darien Project and the Acts of Union with England ensured that they were well supplied with material. A widespread crop failure blighted the last years of the seventeenth century and Scotland's economic position was further weakened by trade wars between European powers; wars in which Scotland was unable to defend itself.

In 1695, the Company of Scotland for Trading to Africa was set up by Scottish financier William Paterson, also a co-founder of the Bank of England. The company's purpose was to extend exports to Africa and the Indies, and the company was established with £400,000 sterling (equivalent to around £44 million today). This investment, raised by public subscription from all levels of society, amounted to roughly a fifth of the country's total wealth. Concerned that the company would damage English trade, William of Orange did everything in his power to crush it. Yet, in 1698 five ships of considerable size sailed from the Firth of Forth, all stocked with various marketable commodities.

On 25 March 1699, news reached Edinburgh that the ships had docked at the Isthmus of Darien (now Panama) and established a settlement, which they had named New Caledonia. There was much rejoicing in the streets and all the city churches offered thanks up to God. But their gratitude was premature, because for most of the hopeful settlers who arrived at Darien, the expedition would turn out to be a disastrous and tragic venture. Agriculture proved difficult, the otherwise friendly natives refused to buy the colonists' trinkets, and William of Orange instructed the surrounding colonies not to supply the Scots. A hot summer caused a high mortality rate in the settlement, with many dying from fever. After barely eight months the colony was abandoned. Of the 2,500 Scots who set off for Darien in two expeditions, only a few hundred survived. This cruel disappointment ruined many families, and the repercussions affected even those who had not invested in the scheme.

As ever, the poor suffered most from the economic blow to the country. Andrew Fletcher, a contemporary author, who co-wrote *A Defence of the Scots Settlement at Darien: With an Answer to the Spanish Memorial Against It* in 1699, explains how the 200,000 poorest people in Scotland survived at this time. Many begged from door-to-door and were often drawn to Edinburgh in the hope of making a living, whether by fair means or foul. The amount of vagabonds, claims Fletcher, doubled after the Darien disaster. Among them, he claims incest became rife, with fathers incestuously involved with their daughters, sons with their mothers, and brothers with sisters. Both men and women were perpetually drunk, cursing, blaspheming and fighting together. Fletcher and his contemporaries perceived the poor as heathens, living without any regard for the laws of their country, nature or even God.

On the other hand, the privileged gentlemen who had lost capital in Darien saw a way to amass new fortunes – a union with England would give them access to all the advantages in commerce the English enjoyed but denied Scots traders. Championing the cause was James Douglas, 2nd Duke of Queensberry, and opposing him the Duke Hamilton, whose ship *The Dowager Hamilton* sank during the Darien venture. Hamilton promised to do everything in his power to preserve Scotland's independence. Many opposed to the union placed their faith in him, but unfortunately, when the time came to vote, the Duke stayed at home with an alleged toothache.

William of Orange was in the process of proposing the union with Scotland to the House of Commons when he met with an unfortunate accident. The king was exercising his new mare, when she stumbled on a molehill and threw him, injuring his right shoulder. The resulting fracture became inflamed, the infection then spread to his lungs and brought on the pneumonia that caused his death on 8 March 1702. According to historian Michael Fry, in *The Union* (2006), William's enemies toasted the 'little gentleman in black velvet' that had built the molehill for many years afterwards. None of the nations forming the British Isles, hated the cold, hard and humourless king more passionately than Scotland. Not only had William done all he could to thwart the Darien venture, his reign had also brought to an end the legitimate line of the Royal house of Stuart and he had ordered the slaughter of every man, woman and child of the MacDonald clan, at the Massacre of Glencoe in 1692.

As William and Queen Mary were childless, the throne passed to his sister-in-law, Anne, the younger daughter of James VII. It would be Anne who made William's wish for a union with Scotland come true. Anne was 37 years old when she came to the throne. She was described as fat, plain and enjoying few pleasures in life apart from drinking brandy in a teacup. It was also whispered by some that she had lesbian tendencies, but if so, she is unlikely ever to have expressed her sexuality openly. After conceiving around 17 times by her husband, the feckless drunkard Prince George of Denmark, only five of Anne's children were born alive. Four died in childhood and the last surviving child, Prince William of Gloucester, died aged 11 in 1700. After her son's death, Anne turned into a chronic invalid in both physical and mental terms.

Although reputedly far from bright, Anne perceived that the Scottish Parliament was a threat to her monarchy. Knowing her preference for Tories over Whigs, the English Parliament held an election after William's death, returning a majority of Tories. The Scottish Parliament was nowhere near so obliging.

Anne knew if a Scottish election was held it would return a parliament with even greater opposition to her sovereignty and her appointment of James Douglas, Duke of Queensberry, as Lord High Commissioner than the current argumentative body. She had to stop or postpone any such election. Instrumental in achieving Anne's desired delay was Daniel Defoe, recruited as a spy by Robert Harley, the Secretary of State for England. Defoe's role was to be Harley's eyes and ears among the Scots. He had to take the utmost caution that nobody should guess that he was employed by the English. To all intents and purposes he was visiting Scotland upon his own business.

The Acts of Union with England were unpopular and instigated nationwide mob violence against 'the parcel of rogues' that signed away Scottish independence for English gold. On the day of the vote by the Scottish parliament in 1707, the Union with England Act was carried by 110 votes to 69. The building and its occupants were stoned by a crowd of men and women disgusted by what they saw as a betrayal. The discontent escalated when Scottish taxes were raised dramatically to support the English economy. The English government wanted to stave off foreign manufacturing competition by hindering the export of raw materials, but the Scottish economy existed on exporting raw materials in exchange for goods manufactured in Europe.

Scots retaliated violently against the excise men, and sold smuggled and illegal whisky stills over the border in England at a profitable rate. According to Arnot, by the end of the eighteenth century, in Edinburgh there were over 400 unlicensed stills. Of the 2,011 houses selling spirits, only 1,600 were licensed, and only 159 of those to sell overseas spirits. The residents of Edinburgh enjoyed the cheap, illicit alcohol and women, although treated as unequal in so many other ways, could match their male counterparts glass for glass. By the middle of the eighteenth century, the Kirk was losing its tight grip on Edinburgh society. Revellers were now ignoring the ten o'clock drum, but it seems that neither the streets nor personal hygiene were much improved. Strolling through the city one night in 1770, Dr Johnson turned to his friend James Boswell and remarked "Sir, I can smell you in the dark".

For the more affluent the list of available entertainments was slowly expanding. Music was especially popular in fashionable circles and, according to Chambers' *Domestic Annals of Scotland,* afternoon 'consorts' were held in the Cross Keys tavern in Edinburgh from 1718. The best Italian sonatas were played by talented amateurs on flutes, violincello and harpsichord. These performances sent an enthusiastic throng of beautiful women into fits of rapture.

Meanwhile, the Edinburgh literati met at the bookshops owned by William Creech and Allan Ramsay, and at parties. Here ladies also enjoyed copious amounts of collops (medallions of meat), boiled fowl and claret. Most flats were too small to hold dancing parties performing the popular country dances and minuets. Nevertheless, at the beginning of the century an old lady Mrs Cockburn, opened up her home in Blair Close to over 20 guests, who danced in two rooms while the musicians played out of a cupboard.

When the feast was finished, the guests rose to sing popular songs, sometimes unaware that the authors were in their company. Miss Jean Elliot listened to her own version of 'Flowers of the Forest' without once claiming authorship and Lady Anne Lindsay sat quietly in the corner when her ballad 'Auld Robin Gray' was sung to the accompaniment of the harp.

The Snuff-Snorting Ladies of the Assemblies

Although happy to dance at parties, most people were reluctant to hold one in their own home. So, in 1710 when the first public assembly opened, and at public balls, Edinburgh Society danced and socialised. After 1720, the assemblies were held at Old Assembly Close, off the High Street, despite the condemnation of such 'promiscuous dancing' by the Kirk.

The assemblies became so popular that dancing teachers started their own businesses, holding events in the bigger rooms of the wynds.

By the late 1770s, the assemblies had deserted the old High Street for more fashionable George Street premises in the New Town. Tickets cost 2s 6d for the dancing, which began at five o'clock and went on till ten or eleven. Refreshments, like tea, coffee, chocolate and biscuits were served. Men also sometimes carried an orange or two in their pockets to offer the ladies for refreshment between dances. The ladies would alternatively suck on the orange and snort pinches of snuff from the dainty boxes hanging at their side.

One of the most well-attended assemblies of the 1750s was run by Miss Nicky Murray, who as self-appointed Lady Directress exercised her strict authority over proceedings. Gentlemen chose their partners in advance, usually at private parties. Another method of selecting a dance partner was for all the ladies to place their fans in a hat; a gentleman would choose one and whoever owned the fan he pulled out was his partner.

While the Edinburgh assemblies were thriving, theatrical productions remained few and far between. In 1736 Allan Ramsay built a playhouse in Carrubbers Close, but the Kirk ensured the magistrates refused the new theatre a licence. Yet, the Kirk's victory was shortlived and plays were soon being performed at Tailor's Hall, avoiding penalties by performing during the intervals and at the end of musical concerts. One of these early plays, staged in 1756, horrified the more staid members of society more than any other. *Douglas*, a verse tragedy, was described as being immoral, irreligious, and packed with impious expressions and horrid swearing. It was not the sort of play one would expect from the pen of a church minister, but it was written by John Home, the Minister of Athelstaneford, who quietly resigned from the Kirk. However, audiences loved the tragedy and at tea-parties ladies recited the opening soliloquy of *Douglas* to their companions and raved over the play. The old bigotry was beginning to lose its hold and eventually in 1764 a licence was granted to a theatre company, allowing them to set up in a field.

The 1756 performance of *Douglas* also featured Sarah Ward, an English actress, who would make a big impact on Scottish theatre. A critic writing in the *Caledonian Mercury* after the opening night on 14 December 1756, applauded Sarah Ward's performance: 'there is no one actress in Britain who could have performed the part of Lady Barnet as well as she has done'. Born around 1727 Sarah Ward, the daughter of an actor, began her theatrical career in York. When only 17, she married fellow actor and minor playwright, Henry Ward. Although their marriage was in some ways conventional, they had two sons and a daughter together, Sarah was free to pursue an independent career and later a tempestuous affair with West Digges, another fellow actor.

Around 1745 Sarah moved to Edinburgh and briefly joined the Tailor's Hall Company but after several disputes amongst the actors, she opened a new theatre in the Canongate, using money raised from public subscriptions and credit from local tradesmen. The theatre was built without legal sanction, but opened on 16 November 1747 with a performance of *Hamlet*. As usual the play was performed under the cover of a musical concert. It was the first building in Scotland built specifically for theatrical performances and quickly established itself as the theatrical centre of Edinburgh.

Sarah Ward's performances established her as Scotland's first female theatrical celebrity, but the actress was not the only woman providing entertainment for the gentlemen of Edinburgh. A far older and more established source of pleasure was thriving in the wynds. At any given point in the eighteenth century, there were hundreds of prostitutes working in the city.

Chapter Six

Women, The Port and Gate of the Devil

This drunken bundle of iniquity, is about fifty years of age, lusty and tall, and she has followed the old trade since she was about 13. One thing she can boast of, that she is daughter of a late worthy Baronet, who was a brave General in the war before last. Being a disgrace to her relations, who are some of the best in Scotland, they sent her to the north, where she continued her business for a long time. She regards neither decency nor decorum, and would as willingly lie with a chimney-sweep as with a lord. Her desires are so immoderate, that she would think nothing of a company of Grenadiers at one time. Take her all in all, she is an abandoned Piece.

(Ranger's Impartial *List of the Ladies of Pleasure in Edinburgh*, privately published in 1775)

John Knox once preached that women were 'the port and gate of the Devil'. Any mention of Auld Nick in a sermon was enough to instil the fear of God into the hearts of the bravest men. But when it came to taking their pleasures, it seems men were only too willing to enter the kingdom of the Devil. The above description of 'Lady Agnew', from *Ranger's Impartial List of the Ladies of Pleasure in Edinburgh*, shows that it was not only women of the lower classes who were practised in the art of giving pleasure. A comprehensive directory and description of all Edinburgh's well-known ladies of the night, *The Impartial List* recommends that, as when purchasing a horse, you should always check a lady's teeth before buying. It also reveals that the prostitutes' trade was highly visible in Scotland's capital during the eighteenth century.

Prostitution was widely practised in Edinburgh, as documented from the sixteenth century onwards. With the parliament and the law courts, foreign ships docking in Leith and single men visiting town and at a loose end, there was plenty of business. The Kirk, always obsessed with the sexual habits of its congregation, claimed that in the Canongate, 'the hail gait abounds with harlotry' in its records. Whether this had anything to do with the General Assembly of the Church of Scotland being held in close proximity to the Canongate, is unclear. It was of course the women the Kirk took its displeasure out on. In 1565 Katherine Lenton admitted to the Kirk Sessions that she was one of many young women who had slept with the French ambassador, while he was in Edinburgh for the General Assembly. Her punishment was to be put in the branks (also known as the scold's bridle), cut on one side of the head and her hair clipped on the other. She was then forced to stand for three hours at the Cross, before being banished from the burgh. If the French ambassador was in any way reprimanded, his punishment is unrecorded.

The wrath of the Kirk was not the only thing that made prostitution a perilous profession. Five years after Christopher Columbus's crew brought syphilis back from the New World around 1500, it was said to be rife in Edinburgh. A cutting from a popular broadsheet, printed around 300 years later, tells of the tragic death of one young girl, presumably from syphilis:

The Life, Sufferings, and Death of Janet Fleming

Daughter of a respectable Farmer near Dunse who was seduced by a profligate young Nobleman-brought to Edinburgh, and kept in the greatest splendour for sometime and then cruelly deserted and thrown upon The town – where, after passing through the numerous vicissitudes of a wicked life she at last fell a victim to disease and died in a noted house in James's Square. With a copy of an Interesting Letter she wrote to her aged parents, a few days before her death – an account of their Visit to her miserable abode, – and a copy of Verses found under her pillow after her decease.

Miss Janet was the elder daughter of Mr Alexander Fleming, a respectable farmer in the vicinity of Dunse. At the early age of seventeen, Janet had the misfortune to attract the attention of a profligate young noble man who happened to be on a fishing excursion in that neighbourhood.

Determined to effect her ruin, he took every opportunity of putting himself in her way; and, by making her numberless little presents, and filling her head with notions of future grandeur, he prevailed upon the unsuspecting maid to quit her parents' roof, and go with him to Edinburgh.

Upon her arrival in town, her noble seducer placed her in stylish lodgings, where she was dressed in the most fashionable manner, and had a maid to wait upon her. He took her to all fashionable places of amusements, and never seemed happy but when in her company. In this manner about twelve months passed away, in a continual round of dissipation, when there appeared a visible change in the conduct of her noble and vile seducer. His visits became less frequent – he upbraided her with extravagance – and she, in return, reproached him with seducing her from her dear parents and peaceful home.

Things went on in this way for a few weeks, when the wretch set off for the Continent, leaving her in possession of only a few shillings, and heavily in arrears with her landlady. For some time she subsisted by pawning the trinkets and other valuables presented by her seducer, until she attracted the notice of a young gentleman of fashion, with whom she cohabited for nearly three months. Left again to her own resources, and descending step by step, she was at length reduced to obtain a livelihood by the casual wages of prostitution; and ran from one scene of dissipation to another, undergoing all the pains of loathsome disease, which persons seldom escape …

At last, worn out by the fatigues of a wicked and vicious life, she lay down on that fatal bed from which she would never rise in life and, conscious of her approaching dissolution, wrote the following short epistle to her afflicted parents; –

Dear Father and Mother. – If you have not altogether discarded from your memory, as unworthy of even occupying a place in your thoughts, her whom you once loved, and reared with such parental fondness but who so vilely repaid your affectionate attentions and slighted your friendly instructions, as to oppress with sorrow the hearts and cover with shame the heads which she was bound to lighten and to honour, you will yet drop a tear of pity on the receipt of this,

Janet Fleming

The town council ordered all those suffering from the 'grandgore' to gather on the sands at Leith for shipment to the island of Inchkeith. It seems this drastic measure was unsuccessful, for the disease spread rapidly through the town, and by the eighteenth century, syphilis and gonorrhoea were widespread throughout Edinburgh. The poet Robert Fergusson, so admired by Robert Burns, liked to write about the street-women of whom he had carnal knowledge:

Near some lamp-post, wi'dowie [gloomy] face,
Wi' heavy een, an' sour grimace,
Stands she that beauty lang had ken'd,
Whoredom her trade, an' vice her end.

It was apparently vice that hastened Robert Fergusson's own death, rumoured to have been from syphilis. Like many others with venereal diseases, he spent his final days in Edinburgh's Bedlam. In 1743 several parishes had pooled resources to build one big workhouse situated near the Bristo Port. It was a filthy and spartan building, housing beggars and paupers entitled to charity, with a special ward for those described as depraved. This bedlam for the insane was hidden in the cellars and it was here Fergusson died in 1774, just after his twenty-fourth birthday.

Lawyer, man of letters and a frequent visitor to bawdy houses, James Boswell suffered several bouts of the Gonorrhoea, which he described as 'that distemper with which Venus, when cross, takes it into her head to plague her votaries'. In his Edinburgh Journals of 1767–1786, Boswell writes of his fear of infecting Mrs Dodds, a lady he has been seeing whilst contemplating marriage to his future wife, Margaret. Mrs Dodds is at this time pregnant:

I am an unhappy man. The consequences of my debauch are now fatal, for I have got a disease from which I suffer severely. It has been long of appearing and is a heavy one. I shall stay a month here after the Session rises, and be cured. I am patient under it, as a just retribution for my licentiousness. But I greatly fear that Mrs – is infected, for I have been with her several times since my debauch, and once within less than a week of the full appearance of mischief. In her present situation the consequences will be dreadful; for, besides the pain that she must endure, an innocent being cannot fail to be injured. (An extract from Boswell to Temple, dated 11 August 1767.)

A Disorderly and Irregular House

Despite the pain and misery caused by sexually transmitted diseases, the number of brothels grew rapidly during the mid-eighteenth century. Rose Street became famous for its bawdy houses, thanks to a Miss Margaret Burns (real name Matthews), who gave notoriety to the street. Miss Burns arrived in Edinburgh from Durham in August 1789 and, together with a Miss Sally Sanderson, took a house in Rose Street. Several complaints about the pair keeping an irregular and disorderly house, entertaining licentious and profligate persons of both sexes, and causing a breach of the public peace followed.

With the help of Burns's publisher, William Creech, Margaret's neighbours took legal action to get her evicted. The case caused a sensation, more so when the defendants were formally banished from the city by the Court of Session. Miss Burns entered an appeal, which was initially refused, only for the verdict later to be overturned. William Creech had been on the bench when Miss Burns's case was heard and he was furious at the final decision. To add to his rage, a London journal joked that 'Bailie Creech, of literary celebrity in Edinburgh, was about to lead the beautiful and accomplished Miss Burns to the hymenal altar!' The publishers later included a statement that they 'now have it on the authority of the gentleman to say that the proposed marriage is not to take place'. Shortly afterwards, Margaret Burns's health deteriorated and she moved to Rosslyn, where she died, aged only 22.

In 1797 the problem of so many houses of ill-repute within the city was acknowledged by the authorities, when Edinburgh Magdalene Asylum was founded. The asylum was established in Gorgie Road, with the purpose of taking whores off the street and training them for domestic service. The institution was a cross between a refuge and a reform school, with most of the inmates aged between 15 and 20. Among their number was one of Burke and Hare's victims, Mary Patterson.

For many years it was believed that Mary had been a well-known prostitute, but while researching her book *The Anatomy Murders* (2011), Lisa Rosner made a startling discovery. As she went through the records of the Magdalene Asylum, she discovered Mary Patterson in one of the pages for 1826. She was not a prostitute but a young girl trying to turn her life around. The ledger recorded that Mary was discharged two years later, on 8 April 1828, just one day before she was murdered by the infamous pair.

From Houses of Assignation to Beer Shops and Low Brothels

By the turn of the nineteenth century, Edinburgh was becoming more cultured – and so were its ladies of pleasure. One church minister is said to have spent a whole afternoon with two such ladies without realising that he was in the company of prostitutes. The inability to distinguish between a tea room and a house of ill-repute seems to be a failing of Scottish church ministers. Dora Noyce, a Madam who ran what she described as 'a YMCA with extras' from her home from the 1940s to the 1980s, complained at being locked up while the General Assembly of the Church of Scotland was in session. She claimed that it was one of her busiest times of the year.

Working girls were not just confining themselves to Edinburgh, but taking excursions to other parts of Scotland. In 1839 many made the trip to the Eglinton Tournament, a medieval re-enactment in Ayrshire. Around half the prostitutes in the city followed the rich to their playground in the west of Scotland. This massive exodus left the brothels back in Edinburgh understaffed and obliged to offer premium rates to new recruits.

Nineteenth century prostitutes may not have met middle-class social and gender ideals of femininity, but they did have a class system of their own, as rigid as that belonging to the rest of society.

A surgeon, William Tait, was the leading campaigner against prostitution in nineteenth century Edinburgh and he describes the intricacies of this system in his book *Magdalenism*, published in 1840:

> *Although circumstances have no doubt a powerful influence in this arrangement, yet natural disposition appears to that which a great measure determines the particular class to which the individual shall belong. Some for example, who commence their career of wickedness in the lowest ranks of prostitution, are unable from mental incapacity or the want of ambition to raise themselves one degree higher, however attractive their figure and appearance may be. Those who are trained from infancy to this life in Blackfriars' and Toddrick's Wynds, are seldom or never admitted into any of the genteel brothels in the New Town. The difficulty of advancing to a more respectable status in a life of prostitution is much greater than many would be apt to imagine. A man may by industry, perseverance, and determination raise himself from any rank of society to another; but this is not the case with a woman who forsakes the path of virtue, and prostitutes her body for the love of gain.*

Tait examined over 200 brothels in Edinburgh, breaking them down into classes:

Genteel houses of assignation	*3*
Second-rate houses of assignation	*15*
Licensed taverns	*10*
Ginger-beer shops	*25*
Genteel public brothels	*10*
Second-rate brothels	*18*
Third-rate brothels	*25*
Very low brothels, eating and lodging houses	*97*

Tait compiled these figures from an exhaustive study of Edinburgh's brothels and the individual girls working in them. So detailed with him. She must have thought that Scott would lose interest in her after her husband's escape had become known. This was not so.

After finally forcing Isabel and her brood out of their home, Scott set the house on fire, burning it to the ground. That night, as the family lay huddled in a nearby barn Isabel gave birth to a daughter. Later, Isabel and her family managed to make their way to France to join her husband, where they lived within the circle of Jacobites at the exiled court of King James. Their ruined house and estate was seized, but the tenants, now forced to pay rent to the Crown, still sent money to Isabel and Ardsheal as well. After Ardsheal died in exile in France in 1757, Isobel journeyed to England in search of a cure for the dropsy. She died at the Peacock Inn in Northampton and was buried in the graveyard of the nearby Church of all Saints.

Not all those committed to the Jacobite Cause were young women. Lady Nairne, a peeress in her own right, was 76 when the uprising came in 1745. The matriarch of a large extended family, she exerted her influence over two sons, four sons-in-law, six grandsons and two nephews, who all took part in the uprising. Lady Nairne was infirm and bed bound when news reached her that one son-in-law was having a little local difficulty with a mob of Hanoverians. She immediately sat up in bed, giving orders for 40 of her retainers to leave for his garrison in Perth to lend him a hand. It was through her daughters though, that Lady Nairne passed on her indomitable spirit. Charlotte, who forced her tenants to join the Jacobite army, and ordered the destruction of their property if they refused, had her own house plundered and vandalised as Cumberland's army marched northwards in January 1746. Another daughter, Lady Strathallan, was around the same time held prisoner in Edinburgh Castle for nine months because of her involvement in the rising.

While many women were supporting their husbands, some acted in direct opposition. In defiance of her husband, Lady Anne MacKintosh raised his clan for Charlie and led many to a horrible death at Culloden. Born Anne Farquharson of Invercauld, Lady MacKintosh came from a strong Jacobite family. Four years before the rebellion, aged 18, she had married Aeneas (Angus), chief of the clan MacKintosh and 20 years her senior. Angus held a captain's commission in the Black Watch and, although he toyed with the idea of rising for Charlie, his plan of action was to sit firmly on the fence, waiting to see which way the wind blew. To his thinking, if he chose the right side then the victor might appoint him overall leader of the clans. His young wife did not exercise the same caution.

Whilst MacKintosh was in London fulfilling his military obligations to the English government, Anne saddled up her horse and rode out over the lands around their estate at Moy Hall. She wore a tartan riding habit and the blue bonnet of the traditional fighting man on her head and spent more than a fortnight rallying MacKintoshes and MacGillivrays to the cause. With her she carried a bag of money and two pistols. She was determined that the tenants were either going to be charmed, bribed or threatened into fighting for Prince Charlie.

One way or another few men could resist her. At the end of her recruiting campaign she had raised 300 men and her bold and decisive action won her the name – 'Colonel Anne'. Anne did not accompany her regiment herself, but she inspected her men before they left for the Battle of Falkirk Muir in January 1746. By defying her husband she had undermined his authority, and acted in an unwomanly way. In fact, she was fair game for the anti-Jacobite propaganda machine and they depicted her as an immensely large and fierce woman.

In April 1746, Inverness was still in English hands, commanded by Lord Loudon, and Anne's husband was one of his officers. In spite of this, Bonnie Prince Charlie decided to stop at the couple's home at Moy Hall on his way to take the town. Anne was delighted to show the prince and his party some Highland hospitality, while they waited for the rest of the Jacobite army to arrive. Anne and her staff provided supper, sherry, claret and entertaining conversation. The household retired to bed on a cold Monday morning only to be woken soon after by news from the Dowager Lady MacKintosh. Lord Loudon, having heard of the Prince's party at Moy Hall, was on his way with a force of 1,500 men. The news caused panic and confusion amongst the guests with people running backwards and forwards, shouting and arguing. However, there was no getting around the fact that a household of under a hundred people could not stand up to so many.

Charles's Adjutant General later sarcastically described Lady Anne MacKintosh as 'running about like a madwoman in her shift'. If Anne's initial reaction was to panic then it was not long before she was able to gather her wits and take decisive and crucial action. Charles was concealed with his baggage by Loch Moy, and scouts were sent out to watch the road and give advance warning of Loudon's approach. A blacksmith Donald Fraser, along with four other scouts, took up positions behind some peat stacks, hoping in the now pitch black night that these would be taken for groups of men. As the government troops approached, Donald and his men ran in all directions, firing off muskets yelling the war cries of the different clans and calling to their imaginary reinforcements, while thunder and lightning raged overhead.

Believing themselves surrounded by the entire Jacobite army, the government troops retreated with great speed to Inverness. The following morning some 200 redcoats deserted, causing so much alarm that the officers decided to retreat still further and wait for the Duke of Cumberland in Ross and Cromarty. Thanks to Anne MacKintosh's quick thinking, Inverness was left wide open and Prince Charlie walked into the town without a shot being fired. The event became known as the Rout of Moy and, whilst nobody was foolhardy enough to mention it to the embarrassed government troops, the Jacobites laughed about it. The trick also earned Anne a second nickname – 'The Heroine'.

Unlike many other Jacobite women prisoners, Anne MacKintosh was never taken to London. She was held prisoner for several weeks and well treated. In fact her needs were so well catered for she was soon able to pass some of her bread to other prisoners. She was then released into her mother-in-law's custody. Despite the strain that the uprising must have placed on her marriage, Anne and Angus seem to have lived happily together. A few years after the massacre at Culloden, the couple visited London where they attended a ball in the presence of the Duke of Cumberland who asked Anne to dance and she accepted. The band struck up the tune, 'Up and waur them a', Willie'. When the unlikely pair finished their circuit of the floor, Anne asked the Duke if, since she had danced to his tune, he would dance to hers. Not wishing to seem ungallant, he offered her his arm as she asked for a Jacobite song 'The Auld Stuart's back again'.

There were no children born to Angus and Anne and she outlived him by seven years, dying in 1787. She was buried by the waters of Leith, her grave sadly neglected over the years.

Jenny Cameron: *Harlequin Incendiary*

If Jacobite supporters celebrated Anne as a heroine, then the popular press of the time saw another unwomanly and decisive female as the Jacobite anti-heroine. Dozens of accounts of her life relate shocking stories and little is known of her real life or whether she was in fact an invented character, loosely based on three different women.

According to contemporary biographers, Jean, known as Jenny, Cameron of Glendessary in the west Highlands is said to have been a spoilt child who lacked parental discipline. Feminine pursuits held no interest for her and she preferred to run wild with her brothers. Jenny was also sexually inquisitive and, at the age of 16, her parents were shocked to find her romping with a boy somewhat older than herself. After this escapade, she was packed off to stay with an aunt in Edinburgh, despite her speaking only the Highland tongue.

This aunt was given a hard time by her charge, though devious Jenny soon discovered that she was more likely to get her own way if she applied herself to her studies and learned to dance, speak French and Italian. As she grew into a tall and striking young woman, her rebellious and wanton side once more emerged and she gallivanted around Edinburgh with her aunt's footman and maid, the two girls dressed in breeches rather than petticoats.

The Wigtown Martyrs Monument in Stirling Cemetery commemorates two young female Covenanters, Margaret Wilson and Margaret McLachlan, who were both executed in 1685 for refusing to swear an oath declaring James VII of Scotland head of the church.

'The devil's picture books': Card games provided entertainment for the upper class ladies of eighteenth century Edinburgh.

(*Above left*) 'Miss Burns' may have been among the 'ladies of pleasure' featured in Ranger's Impartial List Of the Ladies of Pleasure in Edinburgh (1775). (*Above right*) Libberton Wynd, from an etching by Walter Geikie. (*Bottom*) Allan Ramsay's circulating library loaned 'profane' books to the citizens of eighteenth century Edinburgh.

(*Above left*) Lady Grange, Rachel Chiesely, by Sir John Medina. Lady Grange was secretly imprisoned by her husband for several years. (*Above right*) Jane Maxwell, Duchess of Gordon. (*Bottom*) Marriage lintel, Anstruther.

(*Above*) 'Women doing a man's job': Land Girls in the Timber Corps working in Fife during 1940. (*Bottom*) 'The Berry Pickers of Blair': Women and children queue up with buckets of fruit to be weighed in 1952. Courtesy of Special Collections, University of St Andrews

(*Above left*) a woman washing her feet in the Tay at Dundee. (*Above right*) an accordionist in the 1960s. (*Bottom*) This postcard depicting a dour-looking couple is captioned 'The course of true love never did run smooth'. Author's collection

'The First World War left millions of young women sharing an uncertain future': Janet Hunter with her husband, Corporal John Hunter, of the Argyll and Sutherland Highlanders. Author's collection

(*Above*) Women graduates at the University of St Andrews in 1896. (*Bottom*) Winnie Ewing during a visit to St Andrews in 1977. Courtesy of Special Collections, University of St. Andrews

The 'she-cavaliers' and the footman visited all the city's bawdy houses in search of cheap thrills, the two girls apparently enjoying the ladies of pleasure as far as their sex would permit. They were eventually rumbled when arrested at a brawl in one of the brothels. Despite indications that Jenny may have preferred her own sex, aged still only 16, she is said to have then become pregnant by her aunt's footman. As she did not carry the child to full term, it was suspected she had procured an abortion. The scandal brought about by Jenny's behaviour drove her father Hugh Cameron to an early grave and the other members of her family forced her into a French convent to save further embarrassment.

It seems that being incarcerated with nuns did not curb Jenny's sexual appetite. Once more she became pregnant, this time by a Franciscan monk and she had another abortion. Sometime later she met an Irishman called O'Neill and eloped from the convent with him. O'Neill was apparently disgusted to discover that the convent virgin was in fact a sexually experienced woman of questionable morality and discarded her. Despite her loose morals, and alleged tendency to fight duels, Jenny had no difficulty in attracting lovers, and gave birth to a child while still in France. When the opportunity arose to return to her native Scotland, she callously left the child at a foundling hospital on the way.

When she returned home several years later, Jenny is said to have set about seducing her brother. Her sister-in-law is said to have died of shock when she found her husband in a compromising situation with Jenny. According to these accounts, the Cameron siblings went on to have several children together. Then, according to legend, Jenny went on to seduce the 24-year-old Bonnie Prince Charlie, even though she would have been in her forties in 1745.

Jenny Cameron would have been the most fascinating of all the Jacobite women had even a fraction of what the pamphlet press, the tabloids of the eighteenth century, published about her been true. In fact, she seems to have been an eminently respectable lady about whom very little is known. Only three verifiable pieces of information regarding Jenny's life in 1745–6 seem to have emerged.

She was devoted to the Prince and his cause and led around 300 Cameron men to the rallying of the clans at Glenfinnan. She did indeed meet a man called O'Neill and married him. Later she was granted a divorce because of her husband's domestic violence.

The pamphlet writers of Fleet Street and Paternoster Row in London became overexcited when they heard of Jenny's arrival at Glenfinnan. The Jacobite uprising had given them rebellion and violence to report, but the added ingredients of sex and scandal would boost their sales even further. James Ray, a volunteer under the Duke of Cumberland and author of a best-seller about his adventures during the rebellion, wrote a piece, parodying the bible, in which after Glenfinnan Jenny lays certain gifts out for the prince. The Prince with his 'bowels yearning' takes what is freely offered.

Although nobody really knew what Jenny Cameron looked like, hundreds of prints purporting to be of her were sold. Some of the cruder anti-Jacobite prints showed her as a war-like Amazon, others as a full bosomed, shameless hussy.

In 1746 a play, *Harlequin Incendiary or Colombine Cameron* was performed at the Theatre Royal in Drury Lane with the actress Kitty Clive playing Jenny. It was a musical featuring the Pope, the devil, the Young Pretender and Jenny Cameron. The devil was happy to help the Pope cause trouble in 'Old England' but could not leave Hell to stir it up. Instead he enlisted the Young Pretender and Jenny Cameron to do his dirty work for him by starting a rebellion in the 'dreary barren waste' of Scotland's frozen mountains.

Forging his way north in search of retreating Jacobites, the Duke of Cumberland arrested a Jean Cameron in Stirling. Because no one knew what Jenny looked like, he could not be sure he had captured the right woman. Richard Griffiths, a contemporary writer and author of *Ascanius* believed that the woman Cumberland had held at Edinburgh Castle was not the infamous Jenny Cameron, but Jean Cameron, an Edinburgh milliner. Griffiths claimed that due to her sudden notoriety, ladies were flocking to Jean's Lawnmarket shop in order to buy ribbons, fans and gloves. They all wanted to meet Bonnie Prince Charlie's supposed mistress and pick up a little gossip.

It is said that Jenny Cameron could not bear to watch the devastation sweeping through her beloved Morvern and so she went to live in Central Scotland, in the area that is now East Kilbride. She bought a mansion house, renamed it Mount Cameron and turned it into a school for orphans of the 1745 rebellion. When she died in 1773 she was buried on her estate, rather than her ancestral home in Glendessary. Her last resting place has been well-preserved, but perhaps her spirit is still restless so far from her Highland home. Over the years, many people wandering past the spot on a dark winter's night have claimed to have seen a light hovering over her grave.

Anne McKay: *Jacobite martyr*

Unlike Jenny Cameron, there was no doubt surrounding Anne McKay's identity and yet the eighteenth century press showed no interest in her whatsoever. Anne was a Gaelic speaker from Skye, with very little English, which in the eyes of the redcoats made her a savage. When she found herself imprisoned in Edinburgh Castle, alongside Lady Anne MacKintosh, she was not invited to sip afternoon tea with the lady and her redcoat admirers. As a commoner Anne McKay could only expect the most brutal of treatment, and she was tortured. Her gaolers forced her to stand upright without rest for three days and nights as they tried to make her reveal the whereabouts of a young Jacobite soldier she had helped escape from Inverness, after the slaughter at Culloden.

Anne had been lodging with her family at a house in Inverness, whilst anxiously waiting for news of her husband (she would later hear he had died at Carlisle). In the cellar underneath the house, two Jacobite soldiers, Ranald MacDonald of Belfinlay and Robert Nairn, were being detained. The two wounded men had managed to stagger naked into a field hospital, where they were assumed to be Cumberland's men. When the surgeons discovered their true identity, they were moved into the cellar to make way for government soldiers. Anne took care of the wounded men, dressing their injuries and feeding them.

Robert Nairn took a long time to recover from his injuries and was still in Anne's care when he was informed that he would stand trial in London. As he had not only been an officer but also deputy paymaster in the Jacobite Army, he was under no illusions as to what his fate might be. Lady MacKintosh stepped in, and she and her friends hatched a plot with Anne McKay to help Robert escape. Ranald still could not walk, due to his injuries, so he would stay behind.

Anne MacKay put the plan into operation. Having supplied Robert with food and drink and suitable clothing, she chatted to the guard on duty and plied him with drink. When she managed to lead him away from the cellar door and into a nearby close, Robert Nairn made his escape. The English were furious that a simple Highland woman had deprived them of such an important prisoner, and Colonel Leighton of Blakeley's regiment interrogated Anne himself. As she spoke little English, an interpreter was sent for, but neither in Gaelic nor English would Anne reveal who else had been involved in the plot. The colonel resorted to bribery, offering the poor Skye woman a handful of guineas – a fortune for someone in her position. He then resorted to threats, but Anne did not respond. She was then left standing in the guard house for three days, without food or drink, and subjected to considerable verbal abuse by the troopers.

The cruel punishment that Anne received made her legs swell and caused her lasting health problems. Still keeping silent, Anne was sentenced to be whipped through the town and receive 800 lashes for her defiance. However, Lady MacKintosh and her friends intervened, and the beating was not carried out. Instead, after Anne was released, English soldiers visited her house and beat her 17-year-old son so badly that he died of his injuries three days later. Robert Nairn's family fully appreciated what Anne MacKay had done for Robert and they later gave her financial help to bring up her fatherless children and give them a good education.

Many poorer, Gaelic-speaking women who hid or helped fugitives could expect much the same treatment as Anne MacKay if apprehended. Titled ladies, such as Lady Nairne, Lady MacKintosh, Lady Lude, who all played a far greater part in the uprising, were nevertheless treated with far more consideration. Only Lady Strathallan was held for any length of time, and although the Privy Council recommended prosecution for Lady Nairne, then in her seventies, and her daughter Charlotte nothing came of it. This was probably due to Lady Nairne's Hanoverian nephew, the Duke of Atholl, whom she wrote to, begging for clemency for her daughter, Charlotte, Lady Lude, 'a weak, insignificant woman'.

Chapter Eight

The Women who Inspired Robert Burns

Before I saw Clarinda's face
My heart was blithe and gay
Free as the wind, or feathered race
That hop from spray to spray

But now dejected I appear,
Clarinda proves unkind;
I, sighing, drop the silent tear,
But no relief can find.

In plaintive notes my tale rehearses
When I the fair have found;
On every tree appear my verses
That to her praise resound.

But she, ungrateful, shuns my sight,
My faithful love disdains,
My vows and tears her scorn excite –
Another happy reigns.
Ah, though my looks betray,
I envy your success;
Yet love to friendship shall give way,
I cannot wish it less.

(Robert Burns, 'Clarinda', 1787)

By the age of 24, Agnes Broun had spent half of her life fending for herself. She was born the eldest daughter of a small farmer and sometime smuggler, on the Ayrshire coast, an area notorious for smugglers. Aged ten, Agnes had taken on responsibility for her five brothers and sisters when her mother died, leaving her with only the scant education she had gained so far. Two years later, her father remarried, and Agnes was sent to stay with her maternal grandmother, near Maybole in Ayrshire. She was taught to spin and drive the team of plough horses. While working in the fields alongside Will Nelson, a young ploughman, Agnes learned the words to songs, which she would sing to her grandmother and blind uncle.

Agnes became engaged to Will, but both knew that a ploughman's wages would not allow them to set up home. After several years, Agnes discovered that her intended had been unfaithful and broke with him. She was still hurting from the betrayal when she met William Burnes, a gardener, and 11 years her senior, at the Maybole fair. A year later, they married and moved into a cottage at Alloway, which William had built himself. Their first child was a boy and they named him Robert, after his paternal grandfather. Five more children followed, and Agnes was contented with her life and her husband, who was a good provider. She had cows to tend, a manageable amount of land, and her songs.

Most of Agnes's songs were never written down, although a few were printed strips bought cheaply from pedlar's baskets or at fairs. These ballads were passed on via the oral tradition, and often whole verses had been lost and new ones added to fit the old tune. Agnes was a good song-carrier with a voice that was both sweet and strong. Her children loved to listen when she sang, none so much as Robert whose appetite for the old ballads was insatiable. Although his mother did her best to teach him, Robert could not sing. Agnes though, managed to plant in Robert the seed that would grow into a love of collecting old tunes.

Jean Armour: *'a lass that would lo'e me as weel's my dog'*

As a young man, Robert enjoyed a dalliance with dark-haired, dark-eyed, Jean Armour, who came from a respected family within the local community. Her father was a highly respectable builder, a man of substance and Jean's brother Adam was a public-spirited young man who never shirked his duty when called upon to duck a whore in the village pond. The Armours detested Robert Burns, believing him to be a loose and dangerous fellow. This probably made Robert all the more attractive in Jean's eyes.

Jean first encountered Robert at a tavern popular with young men and women during the local fair. There was a dance-floor in an upstairs room where a fiddler played for a penny a reel. The girls lined up along the street on the other side of the churchyard, each waiting to be chosen by a young man who would lead them through the gravestones to the tavern for a dance. That particular night Robert's faithful dog had followed him upstairs and ruined a reel. His comment "I wish I could find a lass that would lo'e me as weel's my dog", caused much laughter among the dancers.

A few days later, Jean was crossing the village green where the women bleached their linen, when she saw Burns walking his dog. She decided to taunt him and shouted "Weel Mossgiel hae ye gotten any lass yet to lo'e ye as weel's your dog?" Although Jean had escaped his notice in the candle-lit tavern, Robert recognised her, and after discovering that she could sing, the two arranged to meet again.

Robert was now penning much-admired verses, and Jean found it impossible to resist him. Despite knowing that Robert had been publicly rebuked by the church for fathering a child by his mother's servant girl, Jean began an intimate relationship with him. In 1785 she discovered she was pregnant. Once again Robert would have to stand before the church court, and as he was fond of Jean he decided to marry her, but not in church. The ceremony would be the simple exchange of consent in front of two witnesses, later converted into a regular marriage by registration in legal form.

On discovering their daughter's condition and the existence of the marriage lines, Jean's parents sent her to Paisley. Jean's parents had persuaded her to hand over the marriage document before her departure for Paisley. If it was legal they could not have it annulled, but after consulting an expert in legal matters, he advised them to remove both Jean and Robert's names from the document, which they did.

Jean returned from Paisley to find a summons to attend the Kirk Session awaiting her. Robert had made no attempt to see her, and she would be attending the Church Session alone. Her pregnancy was now obvious, so rather than be interrogated, she had a statement drawn up revealing Robert as the father of her child, which she signed. Meanwhile Robert Burns had accepted a bookkeeping job on a Jamaican plantation, and it was not Jean he was planning to take with him as his wife, but Mary Campbell, a girl of Highland origin, who had won his heart.

Mary Campbell: *Highland Mary*

Burns first saw Mary Campbell at Tarbolton Church, admiring her habit of locating the chapter and verse in her small bible with a forefinger. She was in Mauchline working as a nursemaid, and came from the Cowal peninsula, on the coast of the Firth of Clyde. She is said not to have been conventionally pretty, but gentle and steadfast. Romance blossomed and Mary agreed to marry Robert and accompany him to Jamaica. Before long Mary knew she was carrying his child and would have to leave her employment.

The pair could not declare their marriage publicly as the church had not yet discharged him of his obligation to Jean. Mary had Robert swear on the bible and they had repeated their vows as they jumped over running water, as was the highland custom. In the autumn of 1786 Mary crossed the sea to meet Burns in Greenock. As she landed, she was overcome with a fever, possibly as a result of premature childbirth and died aged just 23. She was buried in the old West Highland Churchyard at Greenock. In 1920 the churchyard was excavated during the reconstruction of the Harland and Wolff shipyard and when Mary Campbell's grave was opened, among her remains was found the bottom board of an infant's coffin.

Mary Campbell became the subject of Burns's songs, among them 'Highland Mary' and a poem now entitled 'To Mary in Heaven'. Perhaps out of all his conquests Mary Campbell was indeed the one who lived on in his heart. However, undeterred by the tragedy, a few weeks later Burns arrived in Edinburgh, a pony-tailed, buckskin-clad countryman, to share a room with Robert Ainslie, a friend working as a clerk to an Edinburgh lawyer in a Lawnmarket lodging house. Burns was promoting the first Kilmarnock edition of his poems, which had been well received in Ayrshire, and now seeking a publisher for an enlarged edition of his poems. If all failed, there was still his post in the West Indies.

Edinburgh had changed enormously from the city Robert's father had described to him. The New Town was going up, and its fresh architecture was having an effect on the townspeople. Those who considered themselves gentlefolk flocked to the theatre in the New Town, which they considered more Anglicised than the amateur evenings of Scottish music at the old concert-room.

Jane, Duchess of Gordon: *Bonny Jennie of Monreith*

Among the Edinburgh intelligentsia none impressed Burns more than Jane, Duchess of Gordon, a rare female voice in an essentially masculine society. Beautiful, gay and dauntless, the Duchess's broad Scots tongue was notoriously frank and witty. The daughter of Sir William Maxwell, Jane had arrived in Edinburgh in 1760, aged 11. Her mother rented an apartment for herself and her three daughters in Hyndford's Close, about halfway along the Royal Mile.

It was common for Scottish landowning families to rent apartments in Edinburgh, so that their daughters could receive an education before being launched into Edinburgh Society. However, Jane and her sister Eglantine are said to have wandered out into the Lawnmarket and rode on the backs of the pigs, which regularly scavenged the city's streets. While still in her teens, Jane had achieved her own notoriety for her free spirit and beauty. A popular song, 'Bonnie Jennie of Monreith, the Flower of Galloway', was written about her.

After mistakenly believing that her first love, a young officer, had died, Jane married Alexander, the son of the wealthy Duke of

Gordon in 1767. As Duke and Duchess of Gordon after the death of his father, they lived at Gordon Castle in Morayshire, and had five children. Lady Gordon organised parties, planted trees and took a keen interest in farming. She entertained on a lavish scale with sometimes as many as a hundred dinner guests. Among them was Robert Burns, and his first impression of the magnificent residence inspired him to write the poem 'Castle Gordon'. He sent a copy of the poem to Jane, who apparently remarked that she would have enjoyed it more if it had been written in the Scots dialect.

In the 1780s Jane moved to Edinburgh, where she became the leading hostess, giving soirées where artists were asked to entertain. Burns first read his poetry to Edinburgh society in her drawing-room, and Jane became his chief sponsor. The Duke and Duchess moved to London, where they continued to give parties with a decidedly Scottish theme, and featuring country dancing. As King George III adored Jane, she was able to promote her Scottish heritage more than others would have dared, especially after the Act of Proscription, passed in 1746, had banned the wearing of tartan.

By 1793 the army was short of recruits and Jane apparently placed a bet with the Prince Regent that she could enlist more men than he. In order to win, she wore a military uniform and black feathered hat as she toured Scotland organising reels. By this means the Gordon Highlanders, one of Scotland's most famous regiments was founded and Jane won her bet.

Yet, by the late 1790s she was depressed and ill. One of her sons had died young, while her eldest had gone to war, and her husband was living with his mistress at Gordon Castle. Jane would spend the next few years entertaining and throwing lavish parties, determined to arrange good marriages for her daughters.

It is thought that Jean may have enjoyed secret assignations with her soldier lover on the windswept moors. A descendent of the Duchess of Gordon, Sir Michael of Monreith, believes she is remembered in these lines by Burns:

She kiltit up her kirtle weel
To show her bonie cutes sae sma'
And walloped about the reel,
The lightest louper o' them a'!

While some, like slav'ring doited stots
Stroit' out thro' the midden dub,
Fankit their heels among their coats
And gart the floor their backsides rub:

Gordon, the great, the gay, the gallant,
Skip't like a maukin owre a dyke:
Deil tak me, since I was a callant,
Gif e-er my een beheld the like!

But were these lines written by Burns? By 1788 Burns was back at his farm in Ellisland. He had decided to retire from poetry, but he had not given up writing altogether, and undertook some freelance work as a journalist and lampoon writer for the newspapers, under the signatures Agricola, John Barleycorn, Peter Nettle, and Duncan McLeerie. Peter Stuart of the *Star* asked him to become a regular contributor for a salary but Burns preferred to remain an occasional contributor in return for free copies of the paper. He felt the amusement he felt in writing them would cease if he were to be paid.

The lines ridiculing the Duchess of Gordon, quoted above, may have appeared in the *Star,* yet Burns emphatically denied having written the poem for the paper. However, there are some similarities between the poem and Burns's description of the witches and Nannie in 'Tam O'Shanter', written three years later:

As Tammie glower'd, amazed and curious,
The mirth and fun grew fast and furious:
The piper loud and louder blew;
The dancers quick and quicker flew;

They reeled, they set, they cross'd, they cleekit,
Till ilka carlin swat and reekit,
And coost her duddies to the wark,
And linket at it in her sark …

But here my muse her wing maun cour:
Sic flights are far beyond her power;
To sing how Nannie lap and flang,
(A souple jade she was and strang)
And how Tam stood, like ane bewitch'd,
And thought his very een enriched:
Even Satan glowr'd, and fidged fu fain,
And hotch'd and blew wi' might and main;
Till first ae caper, syne anither,
Tam tint his reason a' thegither,
And roars out, "Weel done, Cutty –sark!"
And in an instant a' was dark:
And scarcely had he Maggie rallied,
When out the hellish legion sallied.

Whatever the truth of the matter, the poet freely admitted to using women of his acquaintance for his heroines. Nannie may have been modelled on Jane, Duchess of Gordon.

While in Edinburgh, Burns found himself increasingly uneasy in the polite company to be found in Edinburgh drawing rooms; he began to lead a double-life, gravitating towards more humble society. He became attached to a Highland servant girl, May Cameron, possibly attracted by her frailty and her similarity to his former love, Mary Campbell. May was soon with child and, although he admitted liability for the child's maintenance, Robert seems to have been unsympathetic. He wrote soon after to his friend Robert Ainslie, who had found himself in a similar situation:

I am very sorry for it, but what is done is done … Please call at the Jas. Hog mentioned and send for the wench and give her 10 or 12 shillings, but

> *don't for Heaven's sake meddle with her as a Piece. I insist on this on your honor; and advise her out to some country friends ... call immediately, or as soon as it is dark for God's sake, lest the poor soul be starving. Ask her for a letter I wrote her just now, by way of token. It is unsigned. Write me after the meeting.*

With May Cameron's baby Robert now had four children to provide for and his fame brought him only more adult dependents and a few hundred pounds.

Nancy Maclehose: *The Toast of Glasgow*

Despite his lax morals, Robert was still welcome in Society. At a tea-party hosted by a Miss Nimmo, in Edinburgh's Old Town he met Agnes (also known as 'Nancy') Maclehose, a young, married woman, with a flattering enthusiasm for his poetry, and she invited him to visit her.

At 15, Nancy, the daughter of a surgeon, had been the toast of Glasgow. She was quick-witted and lively and knew how to use her good looks to best advantage. Her father decided to send her to an establishment in Edinburgh for the daughters of gentlemen. A boarding school finish to enhance a girl's matrimonial prospects was the latest novelty in Scotland, and it would also place her out of the way of her admirers.

However, a young Glasgow lawyer, James Maclehose, had booked all the other seats on the stagecoach Nancy was due to travel on, eager to have her all to himself for a day. By the time the coach rolled into Edinburgh Nancy was smitten with him. When she returned to Glasgow six months later, Nancy accepted his proposal of marriage, although her father advised her to wait. Unfortunately it soon became apparent to Nancy that Maclehose was the worst type of husband she could have picked – violently jealous, cruel and a hypocrite.

The couple quarrelled continuously and after three and a half years she left him, returning to her father's home. Maclehose took custody of their children, refusing to allow Nancy access to them. Within months Nancy's father Dr Craig died, leaving her a small annuity, and she decided to move to Edinburgh. Maclehose constantly pestered her suggesting new arrangements, meetings and reunions, and she somehow managed to convince him to let her take charge of their children.

After the break-up of the marriage, Nancy threw herself into strict Calvinism, which had been her mother's faith. However, she also sought the company of the Ploughman Poet. She had read Burns's works and felt that she alone was suited to be his friend, due to their shared experience of misfortune, enjoyment of language and superior minds. After her marriage, Nancy had set about educating herself, studying the best authors in prose and verse, and writing her own poems. Now, thanks to their chance meeting she was eager to befriend Burns and show off her own literary abilities. A prolific exchange of letters began between the two, with Burns signing himself 'Sylvander' and addressing Nancy as 'Clarinda'. Their letters were romantic, a mixture of literature, theology, human misfortune, flirtation, gaiety, although Nancy was determined to maintain a platonic relationship with the amorous poet.

By 1788, 'Clarinda' and 'Sylvander' were still in contact, but the exchanges of letters was less frequent. Robert then decided to lease a farm at Ellisland and immediately saw the need for a wife. Burns could not see Nancy in her feathered hats and ribbons working on the farm, whereas Jean Armour suited his requirements. There was little romance involved in his choice, and Nancy was furious when she heard of his marriage. Afterwards, on a brief trip to Edinburgh he met with Nancy, who seemed to have forgiven him, as he left with a lock of her hair, which he later had made up into a ring.

Meanwhile, Nancy's husband Maclehose was now in Jamaica, doing well for himself. Claiming that he was a changed man, Maclehose offered for Nancy and their remaining living child, to join him in the West Indies. She accepted, and wrote to Burns, commanding him not to write to her in Jamaica, yet wishing him every happiness. She was blissfully unaware that he was now drinking tea with 19-year-old Maria Riddell, whom he had recently become captivated with.

In the weeks leading up to Nancy's departure, Robert had written to her, enclosing three love poems. Despite his inconstancy, 'Ae Fond Kiss' contains some of the most beautiful words ever written.

Ae fond kiss, and then we sever;
Ae fareweel, and then, for ever!
Deep in heart-wrung tears I'll pledge thee,
Warring sighs and groans I'll wage thee.

Who shall say that Fortune grieves him,
While the star of hope she leaves him?
Me, nae cheerfu' twinkle lights me;
Dark despair around benights me.

I'll ne'er blame my partial fancy,
Naething could resist my Nancy:
But to see her was to love her;
Love but her, and love for ever.

Had we never loved sae kindly,
Had we never loved sae blindly,
Never met-or never parted,
We had ne'er been broken-hearted.

Fare thee weel, thou first and fairest!
Fair thee weel, thou best and dearest!
Thine be ilka joy and treasure,
Peace, enjoyment, love, and pleasure!

Part Two

1800–1900

Chapter Nine

With Murder in Mind

A many years ago
When I was young and charming
As some of you may know
I practised baby farming

(Gilbert & Sullivan, *HMS Pinafore*)

Murder is rarely well thought-out in advance, most cases are the result of a brawl or domestic violence. However, women who kill are thought to prefer a less physically violent form of dispatch, such as poison. In the eighteenth and nineteenth centuries poisons were widely available for pest control. One Edinburgh woman, Christian Sinclair, made use of these lax controls to obtain arsenic for murderous purposes in 1813.

Jean Petrie, an Orkney woman was delivered of a daughter in August 1812. The father of the child was a married man also from Orkney, Thomas Sinclair. About a month after the baby was born, Thomas's sister, Christian, called on Jean, bringing her a gift of a little corn. Jean was careful not to mention the fact that Thomas was the father of her child, for fear of annoying Christian, who was known to be a violent-tempered woman.

Christian called again on the evening of April 1813, and, after inviting herself into the house, sent Jean out to buy a bottle of ale while she minded the baby. While alone in the house she force-fed the child arsenic in the form of rat poison. This she had eventually acquired for the purpose, after two failed attempts to buy the poison, first from a woman named Marjory Scatter, who also had a child by Thomas and then from shopkeeper Eric Grant. She eventually persuaded a local cooper, William Petrie (presumably no relation to Jean), to buy sixpence worth of rat poison from Eric Grant, claiming it was for himself. Petrie obtained a receipt for the purchase and two days later he delivered the parcel of arsenic to Christian Sinclair.

When Jean Petrie returned to her house, Christian covered the baby's vomit with ashes, commenting that it had a filthy throat, and warned Jean against letting anyone know of her visit. Concerned by her child suddenly appearing so ill, Jean called in her neighbour, Margaret Ballantyne, who had witnessed the child in good health earlier that day, and John Edgar, a doctor, who administered an emetic. It was too late and Jean's daughter died in agony during the early hours of that morning.

At her trial Christian put up no satisfactory defence, nor could the prosecution find a motive to explain her decision to murder the child. Christian Sinclair's actions were inexplicable. According to a broadside published just after her death, Christian was hanged on 29 December 1813:

> *supported by a man on each side, [she] instantly mounted the drop. The Executioner then placed the Rope round her neck, and gave her a handkerchief, which she was to use as a signal, and which she dropped before he could come off the platform. She was instantly launched into eternity, about half past three o'clock amidst a very great concourse of spectators. After hanging the usual time her body was left down and delivered over for dissection.*

Mary McKinnon: *a murderous madam?*

If Mary McKinnon did indeed stab William Howat on the night of 8 February 1823, then it is hard to believe that she had murder in mind. The events that overtook the middle-aged Edinburgh tavern-keeper, can only be explained by the nature of her profession and the role that alcohol consumption may have played.

In 1823 Mary was around 40 years of age, and she kept a tavern, which also doubled as a brothel at 82 South Bridge, Edinburgh. Whilst she was visiting a friend on the night of 8 February, a party of men, including William Howat, a solicitor's clerk, came into her tavern. After having knocked back several bottles of spirits at a party given by Howat and his house-mate Henry Kerry, the group were all in varying stages of intoxication.

Three young women employed by Mary, Elizabeth MacDonald, Elizabeth Gray and Mary Curly, who lodged and worked at the tavern were, at first, happy enough to see the party and served them with spirits, which they shared with the women. For an hour or so things went well. However, when it was time for the men to leave, some were unhappy with the entertainment they had so far received and ordered more drink. An argument developed and a chair was broken. During the fracas that followed both parties were grabbing at the other, and Howat struck Elizabeth MacDonald on the head.

Mary Curly ran to fetch her mistress, who was enjoying the hospitality of a local grocer, Samuel Hodge, in the Canongate. Samuel returned with Mary to South Bridge, where Mary MacKinnon rushed along the passage to the kitchen, which was now the centre of the brawl. At some point soon after MacKinnon was knocked to the floor and Howat stabbed. As the participants sobered up, they realised that something terrible had happened and the police were sent for. Witness accounts of the incident varied, and while Mary Mackinnon claimed one of the men, John Wilkinson, had stabbed Howat, it was she who was detained at the local police station.

Howat, lying in the infirmary clung on to life for 12 days, before he finally died on 20 February. Ten days earlier, Howat had identified Mary as his assailant from his death bed. At her trial on 14 March, Mary pleaded not guilty to the charge of murder by stabbing Howat in the breast with a table knife. Some of Howat's friends who had been present gave evidence, all backing Howat's statement.

The jury quickly returned a verdict of guilty, with a recommendation to mercy. But after the jury was discharged, the presiding judge stated that he could not discover any mitigating circumstances warranting a recommendation to mercy and he pronounced the death sentence upon the brothel-keeper. Mary was brought to the gallows at the head of Libberton's Wynd on 16 April. Around 20,000 people came to witness her execution.

According to Henry, Lord Cockburn in his diary, *Circuit Journeys* (1888), Mary's last moments were somewhat rare and romantic. Cockburn had been part of the legal team of Jeffrey and Cockburn who had defended Mary in court. Mary had long had a passion for a certain gentleman, who Cockburn refers to as an 'English Jew' and she had asked him to visit her on her last day. He did so and as they were parting, Mary cut an orange in half. Handing her beloved one piece and keeping the other herself, she instructed him to find some window opposite the scaffold where she could see him and to apply the orange to his lips when she touched her own half to her lips. He did so, and Mary died knowing that she was secure in his affections.

Helen McDougal: *The Body-Snatcher's Wife*

People throughout Scotland were well aware of the practice of robbing graves and of felons murdering victims to sell the bodies for dissection. As the Napoleonic wars between 1803 and 1815 escalated, the demand for army and navy surgeons grew in proportion, and hundreds of young men converged upon Scotland's famous medical schools to train as doctors. Each medical student was required to dissect at least one body to qualify. At that time the law allowed only the bodies of executed murderers to be used for dissection, and there were not enough to go round.

Many students despaired of ever being able to take the Hippocratic oath, and some decided to help themselves to newly-buried bodies. Organised gangs of body-snatchers followed suit. Unethical medical schools would pay handsomely for a fresh corpse. It was a lucrative business and not strictly against the law; a body did not belong to anyone, so it cannot be stolen. When the 'sack-em-up' men robbed the grave of its corpse, they left the shroud behind. The shroud was the property of the deceased's family and, unlike the theft of a human corpse, the theft of property was a criminal offence carrying a high penalty.

This method of procuring bodies for medical training caused hysteria throughout Scotland. Burghers defended their churchyards according to the amount of cash available, new technology and fashion trends. Mortsafes, heavy frames made up of iron bands were used to enclose coffins, were common and could be re-used. Mortstones, heavy stone blocks laid over coffins, were also popular. Watchtowers were built by graveyards, and sometimes the guards shot at stray animals by mistake. Sometimes, as in one case in Leith, they shot at each other.

In 1752, the defence team for Helen Torrence and Jean Waldie, who abducted and killed a young boy, could not present any mitigating circumstances at all. At their trial, on 3 February 1752, the jury heard how the two nurses stole John Dallas, aged eight or nine, from his home in Edinburgh and carried him to Waldie's house, where they killed him. The two women then sold his body to a medical school, receiving two shillings for the cadaver, sixpence for transporting it and another ten pence for drink. At Torrence and Waldie's trial the jury found them both guilty of stealing and murdering John Dallas, and the judge ordered that they both be hanged.

Yet, the trial of Torrence and Waldie caused nothing like the panic and hysteria induced by William Burke, Helen McDougal, William Hare and Margaret Hare or Laird. Burke and Hare were Irish immigrants who came to reside in Edinburgh's Canongate, with their respective common-law wives, Helen McDougal and Margaret Laird. Helen McDougal met Burke while she was working as a prostitute, walking the streets of Glasgow. He took her back to Edinburgh, and the couple set up home together.

At some point Burke and Hare hit upon the idea of murdering vulnerable or solitary people and selling them for dissection to medical students. Victims were chosen who would not easily be missed to reduce their chances of being apprehended. However, Burke, Hare and their two female partners were eventually caught and stood accused of 16 murders. Only Burke and McDougal stood trial on 24 December 1828, as the Hares had turned King's evidence, testifying against their former partners-in-crime. Burke was found guilty of just one murder, that of Mrs Campbell (also known as Docherty), a Glaswegian woman who had travelled to Edinburgh to search for her son. After only a few days in the capital, Mrs Campbell's money ran out and she decided to return home.

On the way, she called into a shop in the West Port in search of charity. Unfortunately she ran into Burke, who was also in the shop. Seeing the stranded woman as a suitable victim, he persuaded her to return home with him for breakfast, reassuring her by saying that his mother's name was Docherty and they might be related. At Burke's lodgings, Mrs Campbell was plied with whisky and a great deal of singing and dancing went on. That evening, Burke and Hare pretended to get into a brawl. During the mock scuffle the old woman was thrown to the floor and Burke throttled her. Mrs Campbell's murderers then sold her body for ten pounds.

The jury found the case against Helen McDougal 'not proven'. This verdict, peculiar to Scots law, does not find the accused innocent, but rather that the prosecution has not provided enough evidence to prove their guilt. Testimonies had been given suggesting that Helen had known of Burke's murderous intentions and that she had assisted him in executing the murders by fabricating quarrels, which enabled him to take his victims by surprise. However these testimonies were considered libellous by the court and discounted.

According to a broadside published in Glasgow in 1829, Helen left Edinburgh after her acquittal and made her way back to Glasgow. She had only been in the city a few days before the people she was lodging with recognised her and she was forced to return to her parent's home in Reardon. Her parents, wishing to maintain their respectability were said to have only allowed Helen to leave their home by the back window in the middle of the night.

Helen soon set off for Stirling, where she took up with a native of Perth, a man by the name of Campbell, a spinner by trade. The couple moved to his native Perth, where he found work at the Deanstone Cotton Mill. Again Helen was recognised in the town and decided to seek out Campbell at his workplace. Unfortunately, he was nowhere to be found, and when the mill-workers turned up for their morning shift they recognised Helen. The broadside describes how a great number of the workers, who were mainly women, attacked her. One seized Helen by the hair and throttled her, while another placed her foot on Helen's breast, pressing down until her breastbone cracked. After being carried to a neighbouring house, Helen McDougal died.

After the Burke and Hare trials, the population lived in fear of 'Burking', which became a new term for robbing graves. Despite becoming a legendary body-snatcher, William Burke had always remained adamant that neither he nor Hare had ever robbed a grave. Burke may have been telling the truth, but the panic that ensued after the case played a large part in the introduction of the Anatomy Act in 1832, which allowed medical schools to use bodies from other sources for dissection.

Eight years after the passing of the act, a group of schoolboys playing behind Edinburgh Castle found 17 hand-carved dolls buried in a cave on Arthur's Seat. Each four-inch doll lay within a tiny coffin. People initially believed that the tiny effigies were associated with witchcraft and devil worship, but soon began to associate them with the murder victims of Burke and Hare. It was thought that Burke may have carved and buried the figures out of remorse, yet the identity of the craftsman is still unknown.

Jane Tomkinson: *A Witness to Her Own Funeral*

One Scottish woman claimed to have survived the dissector's knife after her body had been stolen from the grave. Jane Tomkinson's account was published in a broadside by James Mathewson in Edinburgh, around 1825. Broadsides were cheap entertainment and often came from local stories or hearsay, so it is difficult to confirm how much truth these sensational tales contain.

In the account, Mrs Tomkinson recounted how she had fallen into a trance and could not move any part of her body. While in this state, she heard her nurse approach and pronounce her dead, then friends gather around her, weeping. Jane did all in her power to stir, but was incapable of moving a muscle. After a short time a friend drew her hand down Jane's face, closing her eyes. Later, a team of joking and laughing undertakers came into the room and roughly dressed her in her grave clothes. The coffin was brought into the room and the 'corpse' laid in it.

The day of her internment arrived and Jane felt her coffin being placed in the hearse, ready to carry her to her grave. Shortly afterwards, she was aware of being carried on the shoulders of several men, before being placed in a vault. After the mourners left, two people entered the vault and began to break open her coffin. Jane hoped that it was her friends, who, realising she was still alive, had come to rescue her. It was not. Rough hands dragged her from the coffin and then carried her, before she was conveyed some distance by carriage. During the journey, Jane overheard her two kidnappers talking and learned she was in the hands of grave robbers and was to be dissected that night. Still she lay paralysed.

Before dissecting Jane's body, she learned, the medical students intended to try out a new contraption which sent a shock through the corpse. The machine was twice used on Jane and the second shock opened her eyes. She saw the doctor attending her and recognised many students. As the surgeon placed the point of his knife on her bosom, she felt a dreadful cracking throughout her frame, followed by convulsions. The students shrieked in horror as the trance was broken and the 'corpse' sat up on the dissection table.

It is possible that Jane Tomkinson suffered no more than flights of fancy from reading too many broadsides, but there could however, be a grain of truth in her story. Medical students in the nineteenth century are known to have carried out experiments attempting to bring corpses back to life.

Baby Farming in Scotland

With no effective contraception available and pre-marital sex heavily stigmatised, in the 1880s Edinburgh spawned hundreds of illegitimate babies. One solution to the problem of an unwanted baby was to put a sixpenny advertisement in a local newspaper, along the lines of 'Person wanted to adopt child'. Such notices did not go short of replies, nearly all from poor people ready to take the child – for a fee. Some of those who responded were the baby farmers, people who took in children for payment and then killed or neglected them. It was a practice that was to shock and outrage Victorian Britain.

Jessie King, also known as Kean, was orphaned while she was young. She bounced from one institution to another, including the Magdalene Asylum in Edinburgh, before taking up prostitution. Many who had known Jessie believed that she had mental deficiencies ('that lassie was not all there'), and may not have deliberately set out to be a child killer. Instead, some thought she may have been the victim of her heartless and hard drinking common-law husband, Thomas Pearson.

After working as a surgeon's servant and night-attendant at the Montrose asylum in Glasgow, Pearson moved to Edinburgh. In 1887 Pearson and Jessie, who was much younger than him, set up home together in Cheyne Street, Stockbridge. Soon afterwards, Jessie's new baby Grace disappeared and Pearson began making applications to adopt babies on Jessie's behalf. The pair were successful in adopting two boys and a girl, all the illegitimate children of factory girls and domestic servants. Alexander 'Sandy' Gunn was aged 11 months, while Walter Campbell and Violet Tomlinson were just a few weeks old.

Not long after the adoptions, two boys playing together came across a package wrapped in oilskin, which appeared to have been partially burned. One lad kicked it towards his playmate, who opened the bundle then ran for the constable. Inside was the badly decayed corpse of a baby. The police soon turned their attention to the hard-drinking adoptive parents on Cheyne Street. When the house was raided a baby girl was found strangled in the coal closet, while another body was found up on a shelf possibly too high for Jessie to have reached without assistance. Despite the evidence pointing towards Pearson also being involved, Jessie took all the blame and Pearson turned King's evidence against her.

The jury took only four minutes to bring in a guilty verdict and when the judge pronounced the death sentence upon Jessie she collapsed. Despite her institutional track record and statements from fellow inmates that she was easily-led, all appeals for clemency failed. From her prison cell, Jessie forgave Pearson for his part in the murders. Pearson had already returned to Glasgow, where he was to die of a fractured skull in 1890. On 11 March, 1889, Jessie King became the last woman to be hanged in Edinburgh.

Chapter Ten

Dangerous, Educated Women

We, who rally round the Red Flag, are reproached with entertaining the nefarious design of completely destroying the existing order of things; with the desire of totally abolishing the present system of society –for the purpose, it is said of putting some fantastic dream, some wild utopia of our own in place of long established and venerable institutions; the accusers being "bankers, cotton spinners, landowners", as well as "superior women," educated according to the recipes of Mrs Ellis for making "Admirable wives and mothers".

(Helen MacFarlane)

During the eighteenth century, while daughters of the aristocracy were tutored at home, boarding schools were becoming fashionable among the lower upper class and upper middle classes. Edinburgh became the centre of boarding school education, with new schools opening regularly. Most took between six and ten girls, and at first taught a standard curriculum of cooking, sewing, dancing and singing. By the middle of the century the curriculum was changing. Ladies no longer needed to learn to wash and sew, for these chores were now being handed over to servants. By the mid 1700s families were sending their daughters to Edinburgh boarding schools to teach them the urban manners and domestic economy thought necessary for securing a good marriage.

As the century drew to a close, things changed for the worse. Even the daughters of tradesmen believed themselves above any sort of domestic chores and frivolity became the order of the day. Girls took to filling their long hours of leisure with idle amusements. In 1826 Sir John Sinclair claimed that a boarding school education only inspired girls to hanker after admiration and trifling amusements, rather than teaching them how to fulfil the duties of wives and mothers, the primary reason for educating women. Many concurred with the philosopher Jean-Jacques Rousseau, who wrote in *Emile, or On Education* (1762) that women's education should be planned in relation to men, for their principal duties were 'to please men and be useful to them, to win their love and respect, to raise them as children, care for them as adults, counsel and console them, and make their lives sweet and pleasant'.

Few educationalists thought the educational requirements of girls from poor backgrounds worth considering, but George Chapman, the master of a Crieff Academy, offered 'a few hints on the education of women in the lower stations of life' in 1784. Chapman believed that religion and morality were of the greatest importance in life and so future mothers must learn to read the Bible, sing hymns and write. The local parish schools should also instruct girls in cooking, sewing, spinning and knitting, to recommend a girl to a potential husband and to compensate for her lack of a fortune.

The nineteenth century saw great advances in education for Scottish women, although many upper and middle class women were increasingly ornamental, refusing to lift a hand in the house and leaving all the work to their servants. The lady of the house read, sewed, went visiting and undertook charitable work: she could be useful, but in a moral, pious way. Many idle, wealthy housewives endured long hours of tedium and suffered from a type of depression that became known as the 'ennui'. They also suffered from a lack of energy, as they took little exercise and spent their lives in stuffy rooms, wearing constricting clothing.

As the Victorian age progressed, upper class Scottish women's lives became more and more limited. Girls had to be chaperoned on every trip they made and their reading was censored. The jolly, carefree atmosphere of the eighteenth century had been replaced by a dour sentimentality, which saw women turn away from attending the theatre and dances to take up good works. At the same time, more emphasis was put on the need for girls to receive an education suited to their station in life. The ordinary young woman was taught to sew, wash, cook, and read her Bible. They were considered to have no use for any further education. Some were taught needlework, knitting, and other handicrafts in preparation for going into domestic service. One school in Kilmarnock taught the knitting of stockings, not only for the girls' families but to train them as out-workers for the clothing industry.

Standards of literacy increased enormously after the 1872 Education Act made attending school compulsory for all girls between five and 13 years old. Soon, nearly all young Scottish women could read and write, and it became obvious that the girls were quite capable of equalling the boys even in the more academic subjects. In the 1860s many girls attending Ayr Academy, in South Ayrshire, took French and German and, if they chose, were allowed to study Latin and Mathematics.

Helen Macfarlane: *The First Translator of the Communist Manifesto*

Helen Macfarlane was born too early to benefit from the new legislation, but her story proves that it was still possible for women in earlier generations to gain an education. Born in 1818 in Crossmill, in Barrhead, Helen's family were involved in the lucrative Turkey red dye industry. It is not known where Helen attended school, but her family studied dyes with world-leading scientists in Giessen, and while living there Helen learned to speak German, a skill that would later enable her to become the first translator of the *Communist Manifesto*.

However, the Macfarlanes were not oppressed members of the proletariat, but mill owners, and until 1842, Helen lived in a fashionable town house in Glasgow's Royal Crescent. On the death of her father, Helen discovered that the mill was bankrupt, and she and her brothers and sisters were forced to sign away the family house, as well as the rest of their inheritance. Her hopes for a good marriage were dashed and Helen went into service as a governess overseas.

She was teaching in Austria during the Vienna Uprising in 1848. The citizens of Vienna overthrew the government and forced

Emperor Ferdinand I to accept a new constitution. This was later annulled when Ferdinand abdicated the throne and his nephew Franz Joseph was installed to restore the status quo. All this revolution and counter-revolution had a profound effect on Helen and on her return to Britain she began moonlighting for early socialist journals, such as the *Red Republican* and the *Democratic Review*, under the pseudonym of 'Howard Morton'. Her journalism shows that she was one of the first writers to understand the importance of two German thinkers: Hegel and Marx. She wrote of 'a republic without poor; without classes … a society, such indeed as the world has never yet seen, not only of free men, but of free women'. Helen was also a full-blown feminist at a time when even many socialists considered 'votes for women' an embarrassing step too far, and her writing was considered extremist even in radical circles.

Through her articles Helen became acquainted with Frederick Engels, who on behalf of Karl Marx, commissioned her to write a translation of the *Communist Manifesto*, which had first been published in German in 1848. Macfarlane's translation, serialised in the *Red Republican* was hailed by the journal's editor as 'the most revolutionary document ever given to the world'.

After this Helen married Francis Proust, a refugee from the 1848 revolutions, and the couple set out to join her family, who were living in South Africa. Sadly, Francis was not allowed to leave British waters on the emigrant ship and he died soon after failing to board the ship. Their eight-month-old baby daughter, Consuela Pauline Roland Proust, died a few days after the ship arrived in South Africa.

It seems that Helen once again decided to come home, and on her return she married a vicar, the Reverend John Wilkinson Edwards. Becoming a vicar's wife did not change her radical views, but rather added a Christian dimension to them. Helen died, aged just 41, in 1860, leaving behind two small sons, Herbert and Walter. She is buried under a holly tree in Baddiley, Cheshire.

Part Three

1900–1969

Chapter Eleven

The Sweethearts Left Behind

Man's indifference to his fellow man not only wiped out the lives of a whole generation of young men during the First World War, but it also left millions of young women sharing an uncertain future. That generation of women had been taught to depend on men to provide for them, and now all they could rely upon was a letter telling them they stood alone.

By 1914 the population in Glasgow was approaching a million. Immigrants from Ireland and displaced farmers had flocked to what was now the second largest city in the United Kingdom, hoping for a better life and regular employment. Their dreams were rarely realised; working conditions were harsh and poorly paid, and accommodation cramped. The population increase resulted in even greater poverty and disease for most Glasgow residents. Urban expansion had turned the 'dear green place' so admired by writers of the eighteenth century into a stinking black cesspit, unloved and neglected.

The west of Scotland was known as the industrial heartland of the nation, and Glasgow was the key region for shipbuilding, munitions production and engineering. Economic expansion showed signs of coming to an end though with the Great Depression of 1873–96. After a short boom, the early part of the twentieth century saw wages stagnate, while prices increased, and the workers' standard of living dropped. The years 1910–14 saw a massive increase in unrest throughout industrial Clydeside, the result of a combination of factors. For factories to compete successfully in a world market, production had to be re-organised and a greater amount of machination introduced into the work place.

During those four years, the working days lost to strike action were recorded at four times the level for the previous decade. The most famous strike was the industrial action taken in 1911 at the

Singer Sewing Machine Factory in Kilbowie, Clydebank, against pay cuts and workload increases. The strike started by just 12 women brought out nearly all of the 11,000 workforce. Previously acquiescent groups were now unleashing their pent up anger and becoming more radical in their protests against capitalism.

Before the First World War, although many women worked, families were dependent to a large extent on husbands and fathers for an income. The men worked, frequented the public houses, and often spent a large proportion of their pay packets on themselves. Meanwhile, housewives mixed almost exclusively with other women, in a world of never-ending domestic chores. The outbreak of war greatly improved the standard of living for working class Glaswegian families. There was almost full employment, endless overtime and for the first time women controlled the family income.

The war also offered employment opportunities to women, with few men left in their traditional workplaces. Ministry of Munitions figures show that by 1916 there were 18,500 women working in metal trades in the Clydeside area alone. Glasgow was the first city in Britain to recruit women tram drivers and conductors, who were given their own uniform of long green tartan skirts and straw hats. Scottish women took over a variety of jobs as the war unfolded, becoming postwomen, lady lamp-lighters, and meat saleswomen, to name just a few. One canning factory, which only employed war widows, was never short of staff.

Some of the most dangerous work undertaken by women on the home front was in the munitions factories. On a daily basis female workers risked their lives filling shells with dangerous chemicals, like cordite, which gave their skin a yellow tinge that caused them to be nicknamed 'canaries'. Britain's largest manufacturer of cordite was His Majesty's Factory, Gretna, which was built by the Ministry of Munitions in response to the shell crisis of 1915. The factory, which extended over 12 miles, from Mossband, near Longtown, to Dornock, was equipped with a transport network, power source and water supply. Most of the workforce were women, over 11,500 of them, all helping to produce more cordite than all the other British plants combined.

Thousands of women were drafted into the labour force in order to meet wartime production targets. Despite the need for female labour being widely recognised, these women were not made welcome by their male fellow workers or the trade unions. Women took on traditionally male roles in the workplace only for the duration of the war; when ex-soldiers returned they expected women to give up their employment and make way for them. But women had proved that they were as capable at doing any job as any man.

Dr Elsie Inglis: *"No wonder Scotland is a great country if the women are like that!"*

Although women were expected to constantly place themselves in danger during war work such as the making of arms, they were not allowed on to the battlefield even as doctors. One Scottish doctor who volunteered to work at the Front refused to listen when she was told by her local war office 'to go home and be quiet'. However, a government official on the Russian Front would be quoted as having said of Dr Elsie Inglis and the Scottish Women's Hospital Unit, in 1916: 'No wonder Scotland is a great country if the women are like that!' Against the wishes of the British War Office, the Scottish Women's Hospital Unit established field hospitals, dressing stations and clinics throughout war-torn Europe.

Elsie Maude Inglis was born in 1864 in Naini Tal, India, where her father worked for the Indian Civil Service, and came to Edinburgh as a small child. At that time women were expected to mature into wives, and little girls did not grow up to become surgeons. Elsie, however, was a strong-willed child who developed into a tenacious woman and, with the support of her parents, she was determined to qualify as a doctor. After receiving a private education, Elsie put her ambition to study medicine on hold when in 1885 her mother died and she decided to remain in Edinburgh to support her father. The following year Dr Sophia Jex-Blake opened the Edinburgh School of Medicine for Women in the city and Elsie began her studies there.

The two women may have suffered a personality clash, for Elsie went on to finish her training at Glasgow Royal Infirmary, qualifying in 1892. Yet, Elsie was about to discover that, not only was the medical profession male-dominated but the best medical care was also given to men. She was deeply shocked at the low standards of care received by female patients. After a spell as a house surgeon in Elizabeth Garrett Anderson's pioneering New Hospital for Women in London, and then at the Rotunda Hospital, Dublin, a leading maternity hospital, Elsie returned to Edinburgh. In 1894 she set up a medical practice in Edinburgh High Street with Dr Jessie MacGregor, a friend from her days as a medical student, and later a maternity hospital. The medical practice was run solely by women for the benefit of poverty-stricken women. Generous and compassionate, Elsie often waived fees and even paid for women from the slums to convalesce by the sea. The two women struggled to improve the quality of medical care available to poor women but their efforts were hampered by legal restrictions. One law allowed a man the right to stop any medical treatment on his wife, and Elsie constantly fought to have it repealed.

In 1906 Elsie realised that she could not succeed without political action and set up the Scottish Federation of Women's Suffrage Societies. Like her English counterpart Emmeline Pankhurst, Elsie was courageous, audacious and resolute in her pursuit of votes for women. Her autocratic attitude, short temper and rages often reduced her medical and nursing staff to tears, but she was unshakable in her fight for drastic reforms in medicine, as well as equal rights.

On 6 August 1914, two days after England declared war on Germany, the Suffragette movement announced it was suspending all political activity until the end of hostilities, to avoid impeding the war effort. A passive role was not enough for Dr Inglis, however. Elsie wanted to be actively involved in the conflict and she approached the War Office with plans for sending women's medical units to the Western Front. Her offer was rejected, yet she was undeterred. Three months after the war began, Elsie Inglis moved the Scottish Women's Hospital Unit to Abbaye de Royaumont on the Western Front, where they set up an Auxillary Hospital. It was the first of many medical stations staffed by women set up on the Front Line, and financially supported by the National Union of Women's Suffrage Societies and the American Red Cross. Unlike the British, the French Government had been only too happy to accept Elsie's offer.

Throughout the following months, the unit expanded their field hospitals, dressing stations and clinics to the Balkan Front. During an Austrian offensive in the summer of 1915, Elsie was captured but seems to have been repatriated fairly quickly. By August 1916, Elsie Inglis and 80 other women were in Russia, supporting Serbian soldiers. The team of doctors, nurses, cooks, orderlies and ambulance drivers included prominent Scottish suffragettes, like Ishobel Ross and Cicely Hamilton. Evelina Haverfield, one of the leaders of the suffrage movement, was Commandant of the Transport Column and appears to have disagreed with Elsie on the matter of how often lady ambulance drivers should change their clothes. The dispute was placed before a committee and Elsie magnanimously pointed out Mrs Haverfield's wonderful accomplishments, whilst inviting the committee to choose between them. Evelina Haverfield left her post.

Elsie spent only a year in Russia before she was forced to return to Britain while suffering from bowel cancer. She died, aged just 53, on 26 November 1917 at the Station Hotel in Newcastle upon Tyne and was buried in Dean Cemetery, Edinburgh. In the year leading up to her death, Elsie and her team worked in appalling conditions, paying no attention to their own comfort and safety in order to ease the suffering of soldiers ripped to shreds by machine gun bullets and barbed wire. Their efforts to improve hygiene helped to reduce typhus and other epidemics raging through the battlefields. Describing Elsie and her nurses, Winston Churchill is said to have commented, "they will shine in history".

Soon after Elsie Inglis died, the vote she and many others had fought so hard for was given to women over 30 in recognition of their contribution to the war effort. This was a carefully calculated reward that left women in political no man's land. To extend the franchise beyond this would have put women voters in the majority, allowing them the biggest say in the running of the country. They may have played a major part in holding society together during wartime, but women were still not trusted to voice their opinions equally with men.

Chapter Twelve

Glasgow Girls

'Let Glasgow Flourish'

(Glasgow city motto)

Few people today recognise the name Margaret MacDonald if it is not coupled with that of her husband, Charles Rennie Mackintosh. Although Mackintosh acknowledged that Margaret influenced much of his work, his wife's talent has paled into insignificance over the years whilst his reputation has flourished. In one of MacDonald's early works 'The Path of Life' (1894), the elongated forms suggest the designs Mackintosh would later use for his architectural projects and his chairs. Her watercolours present the viewer with choices – to set off on the path leading to all that is beautiful, or stumble down the trail that ends in greed, envy and self-interest. Margaret's work fired Mackintosh with the ideals to develop his new 'Order of Architecture'.

Margaret was not just an advisor, supporter and collaborator to Mackintosh but also one of the most successful, imaginative and technically versatile artists working in Glasgow at the turn of the twentieth century. Her style was innovative and unprecedented. Together with her sister Frances, she produced imagery of the female form labelled 'ghoul-like' by critics. These works were exhibited at the Royal Glasgow Institute of the Fine Arts in Sauchiehall Street and would become central to the avant-garde movement known as the 'Glasgow Style', which dominated the European art scene between 1895 and 1910s.

At this time, Glasgow was the second city of the British Empire. Its coastal location gave it access to international markets in which to promote the city's engineering, textile, ship and locomotive building trades. This new-found wealth was reflected in the need for theatres, public houses and railway stations and those, as well as luxury liners and trains, required furnishings. Some companies had their own upholstery and cabinet-making facilities and the high quality of their work helped to establish the reputation of Scottish firms for stylish furnishings. This demand also created a need for designers. As early as 1840, the government had recognised the selling power of product design and the importance of design skills in the growing economy. Government Design Schools were set up to train designers for supporting roles in manufacturing, and the Glasgow School of Art was founded under this initiative.

By the 1890s the School's headmaster Francis Newbery was also playing a central role in the training of women designers, having increased the percentage of women students. Male dominance in the wider art market was being challenged by the 'New Woman', the name given to women who appeared to be pushing the gender boundaries. With a knack for recognising talent, Newbery was able to encourage the art form for which each student showed the most aptitude. When Margaret and Frances MacDonald joined the school in 1890, Newbery spotted the similarity between the sisters' ideas and those of two part-time students, Charles Rennie Mackintosh and James Herbert MacNair. He introduced the sisters to Mackintosh and MacNair, who were employees of the architectural firm Honeyman and Keppie. The four young artists later became known as the 'Glasgow Four', founding members of 'The Glasgow Style'.

The MacDonald sisters were also influenced by another group at the Glasgow School of Art. One of their fellow students, Lucy Raeburn, published a magazine, which was aimed at the 'new', educated and enquiring woman. Contributions to the magazine came from the MacDonald sisters and other young women, who called themselves 'The Immortals'. The group met at a weekend retreat known as 'The Roaring Camp', in Dunure, a small fishing village on the coast of the Firth of Clyde. On these weekend retreats the ideas that developed into the 'Glasgow Style' were consolidated. The 'Style' came together by combining five established styles – the Spiritualist Revival, the Arts and Crafts Movement, the Celtic

Art Revival, Japonism, and the Symbolist Aesthetic. There is still some speculation as to whether the elongated and contorted human figures within many early works in this style were influenced by the mind-altering states induced by laudanum. The tincture of opium mixed in spirit of wine was rumoured to have been used by the founding artists.

No sketchbooks belonging to Margaret MacDonald are known to survive. She did not usually work from nature, but purely from her own imagination. In her work as in her lifestyle, she sought meaning and truth, expressing both symbolically. A flight of swallows, symbols of the goddesses Isis and Venus signify all that is good in life, while crows or ravens representing greed, darkness and death. The rose motif, laden with feminine significance, also features prominently in her work, for example 'The White Rose and the Red Rose' (c.1902).

The powerful sensual overtones of Margaret's work were a positive influence on Charles Rennie Mackintosh's early designs and became the blueprint for Kate Cranston's Willow Tea Rooms, in Glasgow, which Mackintosh designed. Around 1911, Mackintosh's work became heavier and more masculine, while Margaret's few embroidery designs had begun to show a bolder sense of colour. Margaret's last watercolour the dramatic 'La Mort Parfumee' (1921) is one of her most challenging pieces. Her antimacassar (cloth chair cover) design for Hill House in Helensburgh, one of Mackintosh's commissions, shares common principles with the work and teaching of Jessie Newberry, Glasgow School of Art's embroidery teacher.

Charles Rennie Mackintosh died from cancer in 1928 and Margaret lived for another five years. When she died in her Chelsea studio in January 1933 only a small article in *The Times* marked her passing. Perhaps Glasgow, so proud of its emblem of the tree, bird, fish, and bell, and its motto 'Let Glasgow Flourish', will one day celebrate the life of a woman who contributed so much to its reputation as a city of culture. Rather than allow Margaret

MacDonald's work to pass into obscurity, it might be fitting to commemorate her with an epitaph to be found in James Herbert McNair's 1896 bookplate design, 'The Tree of Knowledge':

Nourished by Middle Earth,
Breathed on by Heavenly Dew,
Flourished a Tree of Worth,
Flourished and Grew
The Tree of Knowledge.

Chapter Thirteen

Reforming Women

What we have done for ourselves alone dies with us.
What we do for others and the world remains, and is immortal.
(Albert Pike, *Ex Corde Locutiones*)

During the First World War, the Liberal Prime Minister David Lloyd George, promised a nation living in squalor 'Homes for Heroes'. It was a promise that he would not keep. Not until the Labour Party came to power in 1924 was a budget allocated for building new homes. However, at a time when women had little or no say in political reform, one Glasgow housewife, Mary Barbour, was instrumental in improving the living standards of the city's tenement dwellers.

Tenements symbolised Scotland's traditional connection with the continent, as they were built to the same design as European urban housing. Most were four storeys tall, and solidly built of stone, and they offered flexible living accommodation behind their handsome street façades. Up to 12 families shared each tenement close or community entrance, most living in just a single room, or a room with a kitchen. All households would share a privy, or dry toilet, and a green, where they could dry their washing. Some tenements had shops on the ground-floor, ensuring that no one had to travel far for their groceries and locals became well-known to the shopkeepers.

A surge in Glasgow's population due to industrialisation during the nineteenth century led to overcrowding in inner-city areas. In response, the corporation built the 'Backlands', new tenements filling the spaces between existing buildings and blocking out sunlight and air. The new tenements were so close together that neighbours could reach out of the window and touch the hand of a person in the opposite tenement. Philanthropic organisations, like

'Fresh Air Fortnights' sprang up to subsidise holidays at the seaside or in the country to improve the health of poor children.

Only token measures were taken to control these increasingly unhealthy living conditions. The Glasgow Police Act of 1866 gave the Town Council the power to inspect homes that consisted of three rooms or less. Tickets placed by the council inspectors on the front doors gave the cubic capacity of the dwelling and the number of people legally allowed to sleep in it. One-room flats, known as 'single-ends', could be as small as 14 feet by 11 feet and might accommodate a family of ten or more. In many homes, lodgers brought in extra income and beds could be worked on a shift basis.

One feature of the tenement apartments was the 'set in', a hole in the wall bed, which could accommodate up to eight people lying top-to-tail. These boxed beds were often built as bed closets, beds in cupboards with a door. In 1900 city councillors had realised that proper ventilation was crucial to public health and brought in the Glasgow Building Regulations Act banning 'set in' beds, and forcing landlords to comply with these regulations within five years.

No matter how many were squeezed into the small living area, there was always room for more. New Year's Eve celebrations might see as many as 40 people packed into a small apartment. Despite the poverty within Glasgow's tenements, Hogmanay was a continuous round of singing, dancing, eating and sociability. Men would save for a half bottle of whisky and visit friends at midnight to share drinks, following the tradition of first-footing (the first person to cross the threshold of a dwelling on New Year's Day, bringing luck to a household). According to tradition, to be first over the threshold in the New Year, a man had to be dark-haired and carry a piece of coal to bring prosperity. Unlucky fair-haired men might be asked to come back later.

Cleanliness within tenement homes was a point of honour for most and their solid stone structures ensured that the coal fires kept homes warm and cosy. Most of the inhabitants were also aware of the value of fresh air. Children were walked in their prams or left outside the close to take the air, and older children were sent outside to play. Windows were constantly flung open, so that mothers could shout down to children playing in the back yard to come in for their tea or to throw a piece of bread down to a child shouting for 'a piece an' sugar'. 'Hinging oot the windae' was also a popular pastime. Although considered common by those who thought themselves respectable, it enabled women stuck indoors all day to relax and watch what the neighbours were up to. Windows were also used to make a point in an argument. After trading insults the window could be slammed, enabling the slammer to have the last word.

By the First World War, the Glasgow tenement buildings were in need of extensive repairs and there was no government money left over from the war effort to maintain homes. The crumbling state of buildings did not, however, stop landlords from raising rents and evicting those who could not pay. The women of Glasgow began to put notices in their windows declaring a rent strike. If the sheriff's officers were due to make an eviction, the local women would warn each other of their arrival by banging pots and pans, ringing bells and blowing trumpets. The officers would meet a barricade of women waiting for them in the close, throwing missiles of flour meal and whiting. Few officers found the courage to tackle them.

After the success of the Glasgow Women's Housing Association, which was formed in 1914 to oppose the wartime rent rise, political activist Mary Barbour set up a sister organisation, the South Govan Women's Housing Association. Through networking between several organisations, including the Women's Co-operative Guilds and the Social Sunday School Movement, Mary was able to organise Glasgow's women into one body. On 17 November 1915, thousands of women marched through the city's streets, from Glasgow Green to the Sheriff Court.

The pressure Mary and her followers, nicknamed 'Mrs Barbour's Army', put on the government brought about the Rent Restriction Act, which fixed rents at pre-war levels and benefited the whole country. Just over seven decades later their tactics would inspire successful opposition among Glaswegian citizens to the Poll Tax introduced by Margaret Thatcher in 1989. Once again notices sprang up in windows, declaring 'No Poll Tax Here' and the Strathclyde Anti-Poll Tax Federation determined that no one had their goods seized for non-payment in the Strathclyde area.

Glasgow's city planners did not consider rehousing the tenement dwellers until the Scotland Housing Act of 1930. The long awaited 'homes for heroes' projected after the First World War became the Blackhill housing scheme, cheaply-built houses miles from the city centre, without shops, public transport or any other amenities nearby. The Second World War saw the tenements deteriorating once again for want of maintenance and many collapsed. Some tenement dwellers were not rehoused by the council until the 1950s. By then each new home had running water and a bathroom, but the self-supporting community that had thrived in the tenements, due to the help of women like Mary Barbour was gone forever. People were split from their families and old neighbours and became isolated.

Cod Liver Oil and Condensed Milk

With only a little money to feed their families, many tenement women always had a pan of warm and filling soup or porridge simmering on the stove. Peaky-looking children were treated to tonics such as cod liver oil and condensed milk. Although rich in vitamin A and D these tonics were not enough to combat the bone-deforming disease rickets. A large percentage of tenement children suffered from rickets due to a lack of sunlight and a deficiency of foods such as oily fish and eggs.

After being elected Glasgow's first woman Independent Labour Councillor, in 1920, rent campaigner Mary Barbour, introduced a scheme where school children were given a free bottle of milk a day to ensure they received the basic vitamins they needed. By the 1940s cereal and margarine makers saw the benefits of supplementing everyday foods with Vitamins A and D and began adding them to their products. The Independent Labour Party's dream of a free health service was realised in 1947, with the establishment of the NHS, and gradually the health of Glasgow's children improved.

In her long career, Mary Barbour pushed through many policies to help working class communities. During the years 1924 to 1927, she served as Glasgow Corporation's first woman baillie, and was one of the first female magistrates in the city. Mary's work allowed her to develop her commitment to the welfare of women and children and in 1925 she was appointed chairperson of the Women's Welfare and Advisory Clinic, Glasgow's first family planning centre. She helped to introduce child welfare centres, play areas, and pensions for mothers, as well as building more public baths and laundries.

Mary Barbour retired from her council work in 1931, but she remained active in the local Co-operative societies. In her later years she was still involved in welfare work and organised trips to the seaside for poor children. When Mary Barbour died aged 83, on 2 April, 1958, no headstone was erected to commemorate her life and work. She was cremated at Craigton Crematorium, in Govan. However, Mary's legacy lived on. As the ancient Greek statesman Pericles once said, 'What you leave behind is not what is engraved in stone monuments, but what is woven into the lives of others'.

Chapter Fourteen

A Vital Spark

Workers of all lands unite!

(Karl Marx and Fredrich Engels,
The Communist Manifesto, 1848)

Miss Jean Brodie is one of the most complex characters in modern literature. A teacher at the Marcia Blaine School for girls in 1930s Edinburgh, Miss Brodie's methods are frowned upon by her headmistress. Jean is passionate about her girls, especially the handful she has singled out for special attention. Her influence on her pupils, however, is destructive rather than nurturing. She attempts to cajole one of her girls, Sandy, into an affair with the art master, and influences another, Mary McGregor, into joining her brother, who is fighting in the Spanish Civil War. Mary, a shy and naïve girl, departs for Spain to join General Franco's Fascist army, as she wishes to impress Miss Brodie, who is a great admirer of Hitler and Mussolini. Mary reaches Spain but is killed in a train crash before she can discover that her brother is fighting, not for General Franco but the Republican forces.

Muriel Spark created the character of Jean Brodie in her novel *The Prime of Miss Jean Brodie* (1961). Within the book she adeptly draws out a very Scottish theme, that of good and evil and the inability for one to exist without the other, personifying this in the character of Jean. Spark attended James Gillespie's High School for Girls, in Edinburgh, and she used the school and one of her own teachers, Christina Kay, as inspiration for the novel.

Christina Kay was born in 1878, at 4 Grindlay Street Edinburgh and she lived for most of her life in the same flat. She remained a class mistress during her career at the James Gillespie's High School and appeared to lead an uneventful life. Behind her ordinary appearance though, Christina and Jean shared many experiences and traits. Both lost a fiancé in the First World War, and, like her fictional counterpart, Christina regaled her girls with stories of her trips to foreign parts, mainly Italy and the fine art she saw there. She spoke in dazzling non sequiturs and referred to her class as the 'crème-de-la-crème'. Favourite pupils, including Muriel Spark, were treated to trips to the ballet, exhibitions and theatre, to develop their cultural interests. Like Jean, Miss Kay was also an admirer of fascist regimes.

In creating the unworldly character of Mary MacGregor, Spark drew on the experiences of real Scottish women who went out to Spain during the Civil War, but then she turns the truth on its head. Although some women, like Mary MacGregor, travelled to Spain to fight, more became nursing volunteers, and flocked to the battle sites, driven by humanitarian instincts. Trained nurses, ambulance drivers and doctors, all offered their services. One of the first British women to be killed was an artist. Felicia Browne had been visiting Barcelona to paint, and when the fighting broke out she enrolled in a communist militia and died in action on the Aragón front, in 1936.

One Scottish volunteer, Sister Winifred Wilson, from St Andrews was angered into lending her skills by the inaction of the non-interventionist British Government. In a letter home, she described the violence she had witnessed:

> *After an attack we are working day and night. Oh if you only saw the slaughter! Heads and faces blown to bits, stomachs and brains protruding, limbs shattered or off. They need our help, poor people, and if you could only see them when bombs are dropping overhead, I can vouch your heart would ache. Mothers snatch their children and run madly for shelter.*

In Edinburgh too, fascism had been making its presence felt. A huge rally was held by 'Blackshirts' at the Usher hall in 1934 with Sir Oswald Mosley as their main speaker. The cause of the Spanish Republicans seemed to strike a chord with Scotswomen on several levels. They responded sympathetically to atrocities pictured in cinema newsreels by pledging to act for the Republican casualties in Spain. After all, hunger, poverty and exploitation were things that they were only too familiar with. A form of international female solidarity existed too. As the cause of the Republicans was the cause of Spanish women, it was the cause of women everywhere.

Women fought alongside men in the people's militias, which had sprung up at the beginning of the war. For many Scottish women used to playing only supporting roles in the dramas staged by men in Trade Union Halls, Republican figureheads, like Dolores Ibüürruri Gómez, must have been a symbol of hope and inspiration. Known as 'La Pasionaria', Dolores was born a miner's daughter yet she became vice-president of the Spanish Communist Party in 1937 and played a vital role during the Civil War.

Mary Docherty: '*a Citizen of the World*'

Mary Docherty was among the Scotswomen who volunteered to fight in Spain with the International Brigade in 1937. She was turned down as she had no nursing experience, but undeterred Mary set about raising money for medical supplies and collecting food for the 'Aid Spain' campaign. Although there was a high rate of unemployment in her home town of Cowdenbeath, people with little themselves gave generously.

In her autobiography, *A Miner's Lass* (1992), Mary describes the poverty and hardship that existed in the Fife mining towns at the turn of the twentieth century, the exploitation of women workers and her reasons for becoming a life-long member of the Communist Party. Mary was born in 1908, at a time when the livelihoods of whole communities depended upon the pits where the miners lived and worked in oppressive conditions and had few rights. Mine workers chipped away at the coal face with picks and shovels, tying string under the knees of their trousers to keep the rats from running up their legs.

Men worked eight hours a day, six days a week, and were paid 1s 6d per ton of coal they sent to the surface. If too many stones were found in that coal then the miner responsible would be fined. They paid for their own tools, as well as for the explosives used to blast the coal face. This practice resulted in many big falls and injuries amongst the miners who had little chance of receiving compensation from the mine owners. Such dangerous and dirty conditions caused much anger amongst the workers and trade unions grew in power and influence. From the beginning of the century to the General Strike in 1926 numerous strikes attempted to gain better working conditions.

When the men walked out, it fell to the womenfolk of the town to find the money to feed the hungry families. During the nineteenth century women too worked down the pits, carrying the coal up to the surface on their backs, until they were replaced by pit ponies. Single women still worked at the pithead, loading the wagons and sorting and cleaning the coal. The lack of health and safety procedures made the pithead just as dangerous a place to work as the underground mine.

According to the National Database of Mining Deaths, 21 women and girls were killed at pitheads in Fife during the years 1851–1914. Among them was Ann Japp, aged 14, a pithead assistant at the Dundonald Pit in Auchterderran, who was killed in 1877 when she fell down a mine shaft, while attempting to load an empty hutch onto a cage. In 1906 Mary Lynch, a 17-year-old coal cleaner, was working at a picking table at the Michael Pit in East Wemyss. She broke her neck when she overbalanced and fell into a revolving shaft which caught her clothing. Other non-fatal accidents could disable mine workers. In 1890, 57-year-old Margaret Bissett was run over by a wagon whilst working as a trimmer at the Townhill Pit, and her leg had to be amputated.

Most married women relied on their husband's wages and when pit workers were out on strike women like Mary Docherty's mother had to take any work they could find, cleaning or taking in washing to earn a few shillings to put a pot of Scotch broth on the table. For most of the time that Mary's mother was pregnant with her in 1907–8 her father was on strike, and the couple lived on the herring sold cheaply by local fishwives. As a result of Mrs Docherty's poor diet, Mary was a small baby. She was also born with a predisposition to the tuberculosis, which would plague her teenage years.

Despite the Docherty family's poverty, Mary recalls her childhood fondly in her memoirs. In some ways, she points out, children growing up in the Scottish mining towns had an idyllic childhood with the freedom to pick wild flowers and run through the fields barefoot in the summer months. Pocket money could never be taken for granted, but when a child was given a penny the local sweetshop counter offered an exciting banquet of toffees, jube jubes, sherbet dabs, aniseed balls, sugar mice and lucky bags to choose from. Enterprising children joined the rats in rummaging through the smouldering ashes of the local rubbish tip in search of any still useful items.

Christmas presents were few and far between for Mary. Writing decades later, she remembered the morning when she stopped believing in Santa Claus. Her mother had always told her that if she did not sleep, Santa would not leave any presents for her. When Mary and her sisters woke on Christmas morning that year, over-excited, they jumped out of bed to check the stockings they had hung up the previous night. There were no presents inside.

The people of Cowdenbeath, like many small towns enduring hardship, formed a close and supportive community. The local theatre put on variety shows, pantomimes, dramas and operas starring famous performers of the day, and locals who could not afford tickets were sometimes allowed in free by the staff. Other entertainment was provided through amateur dramatics and concerts, many put on by the Temperance Society, where those who could sing or recite poetry would entertain their neighbours.

On Sundays many children went to the Sunday Schools run, not only by the Church, but also by political movements. In Cowdenbeath Mary attended a popular Sunday school set up by the Independent Labour Party (ILP). Writing in 1991, Mary could still remember all the songs that she sang at these Sunday meetings, including the following, part of a 'Socialist Ten Commandments' taught in some socialist Sunday schools:

Thou shalt inscribe on your banner;
"Workers of All Lands Unite"
You have nothing to lose but your chains:
You have a world to win

Thou shalt not be a patriot;
For a patriot is an International Blackleg
Your duty to yourself and your class
Demands that you be a citizen of the World.

Thou shalt not take part in any bourgeois war
For all modern wars are the result of the clash
Of economic interest
Your duty as an internationalist is to wage class war
Against all such wars.

Winters were cold and hard and although many children went to school barefoot, Mary and her sisters were always kept from class when they were without shoes to wear. Like many girls of her generation, Mary did well at school but was forced to leave at 14 for economic reasons. It took some time for her to find a job and for a while she helped her father sell bread rolls, as he was now blacklisted by local mine owners for inciting workers to strike. While delivering rolls to the Buttercup Dairy Shop, Mary was offered her first job working on Saturday mornings. She and two other girls carried two heavy baskets filled with margarine, butter, eggs and other dairy products around the streets of Crossgates.

Yet, the General Strike of 1926 found Mary once more unemployed. Cowdenbeath was hit hard by the strike and many women relied on soup kitchens, for the striking miners' wives were ignored by the local parish council when they gave out financial relief. A protest march to Dunfermline was organised, in which women and children walked to the poor house and begged to be admitted. As they knew, the building could not accommodate the hundreds on the march and the local parish councils were forced to give each family a little money.

During the 1926 strike, concerts and social events were arranged by the local branch of the Communist Party to keep morale up. At one of these events in the local Co-operative hall Mary and her friend Jessie applied to join the Communist Party. From the day she received her card Mary was an active member in promoting the party. As well as taking charge of producing the party literature for Fife, Mary organised the children's section of the party, teaching revolutionary songs, poetry and organising plays staged at propaganda meetings. In 1928 she organised a 'school strike' for May Day and was successful in obtaining a holiday for the children on the first of May each year from 1929, the same year as the parliamentary elections.

She also campaigned tirelessly for J.V. Leckie, the Communist Party candidate for Dunfermline Burghs, although he did not win the seat. Leckie was the National Organiser for the Worker's International Relief and when he set up a branch in Fife Mary was one of the Cowdenbeath women he recruited to collect sacks of clothes for children in need. Despite her heavy workload Mary was often going without food and her health deteriorated. She developed a swollen gland in her neck which turned out to be tubercular, and required operations.

Mary had been selected by the Youth Communist League as a delegate on a visit to the Soviet Union. Mary was waiting to have a second operation to remove a tubercular growth and the party persuaded her not to wait, but to go to Russia instead, assuring her that the party would look after her. In Leningrad and Moscow, Mary enjoyed trips to national landmarks, like the *Aurora*, the first ship to fire a shot on the Winter Palace in the 1917 revolution. Whilst attending the Children's International meeting in the Lenin stadium she saw Lenin's wife, Krupskaya, and Leo Tolstoy, the author of *War and Peace*. Towards the end of her trip, the tuberculosis struck again and she was sent to a sanatorium near the Black Sea, where she was given the best medical treatment available. Mary received daily injections, special baths and sun-ray treatment, plenty of bed rest and built up her strength with four good meals a day.

After she returned to Scotland Mary's tuberculosis never returned. However, Mary began to discover that her trip to the Soviet Union restricted her from finding work. When she applied to the Servants Register in Edinburgh, a prospective employer found out about her Communist Party background and complained to the agency. The agency told her that she would have to take a job that did not require references and this meant working in a hospital. Mary found a job as a cleaner working in the nurses' quarters of Leith Hospital.

Each day she started at 6.30am and did not finish her duties until 9pm, and she only had one half-day a week and every third Saturday off. She was only paid two pounds a month, as her meals were supplied. The food was poor and the portions meagre, with breakfast consisting of bread with barely enough margarine to cover it. The girls were not allowed to begin their meal until sister said grace and Mary strongly objected to having to thank God for the food that she had worked hard for.

After leaving Leith Hospital, Mary was once more unemployed. As she was still sending money home to her family, she found herself living off water and a two-pence bar of chocolate a day. Before long she found a job as a general servant for two sisters and their brother. She stayed for five years and for every one of them she hoped that she would not still be there the following Christmas. The family she worked for would invite up to 12 people to Christmas dinner and Mary was expected to cook, serve, wash up and wait table all on her own. The dinner consisted of fish, followed by soup, then turkey, potatoes and vegetables, followed by trifle, mince pies, plum pudding, sweets, nuts and raisins, and finally coffee and biscuits to finish. She could only manage to grab handfuls of nuts in passing, for as soon as one course was delivered to the dining room another was waiting to come out of the oven, and meanwhile the pile of washing-up in the sink was growing. To thank her, the family never forgot to buy Mary a Christmas present: every year she received a new overall.

News of her mother's ill health took Mary back to Fife. On her return to Cowdenbeath she found a job with the local dentist. The work was heavy and included cleaning out the spittoon the patients used to rinse their mouths. Despite the long hours, Mary picked up her Communist Party activities where she had left off. She resumed charge of literature and the children's section, but now she also collected money for party causes.

For Mary, there was only a brief respite between the end of the Spanish Civil War on 1 April 1939 and the radio broadcast on 3 September 1939 by Prime Minister Neville Chamberlain, announcing that the British people were now at war with Nazi Germany. Scottish women would have fresh battles to fight on the Home Front in the six years to follow.

Chapter Fifteen

Scotland's Last Witch

At the conclusion of the fourth seance we led the medium to a settee and called for the apparatus. At the sight of it, the lady promptly went into a trance ... [then] Mrs. Duncan, without the slightest warning, dashed out into the street, had an attack of hysteria and began to tear her seance garment to pieces. She clutched the railings and screamed and screamed. Her husband tried to pacify her. It was useless. I leave the reader to visualize the scene. A seventeen-stone woman, clad in black sateen tights, locked to the railings, screaming at the top of her voice.

(Report by investigator Harry Price
on the mediumship of Helen Duncan)

In 1735 King George II reformed the notorious Elizabethan Witchcraft Act of 1563. Under the new legislation a culprit could no longer be executed for consorting with evil spirits. Anyone who claimed to have the power to cast spells, call up spirits or look into the future was now to be tried as a vagrant and punished with a fine or period of imprisonment. At the time of the Enlightenment one might have thought that such archaic laws would have become obsolete. The 1735 act, though, would linger until 1951, and during the Second World War was used by the English wartime security services, as they conspired to silence a housewife from Perthshire.

Helen Duncan, the daughter of a master cabinet-maker was born in the small town of Callander on 25 November 1897. She married Henry, another cabinet-maker, bore him six children and worked part-time in the local bleach factory to make ends meet. Helen was by all accounts a kindly and generous soul, and although she too was poverty-stricken, she often helped to pay her destitute neighbours' medical bills.

In many ways she was a typical Scots housewife of her time, yet unlike most Scots housewives Helen discovered that she had a rare psychic gift: she was able to transport the dead back to communicate with their relatives. Spirits materialised in the form of ectoplasm, which emerged from Helen's mouth while she was in a state of trance.

During the interwar period the popularity of séances had escalated, and between 1914 and 1918 the number of spiritualist societies reached an all time high. By the 1930s Helen was well established as a medium and within a few years she was travelling the length and breadth of Britain, comforting thousands of grieving families. However, her abilities would get her into trouble during the Second World War. The government did not officially class spiritualism as a threat to security, yet for some reason the War Office feared that Helen would divulge the dates of the forthcoming Normandy Landings.

There is no evidence that Helen had ever claimed to foresee the future, but after a sitting in Edinburgh, on 24 May 1941, she came to the attention of the security services. Albert, Helen's spirit guide, announced that the Royal Navy battle cruiser HMS *Hood* had sunk during the Battle of Denmark Strait two hours earlier; something she could not possibly have known. Brigadier Roy Firebrace, then Chief of Security in Scotland and an enthusiastic believer in spiritualism, was at the meeting. He immediately rang the Admiralty who denied the loss, then a few hours later Firebrace received a phone call informing him HMS *Hood* had indeed gone down at 1.30 pm that afternoon.

It was not her revelation about HMS *Hood*, but the words of a deceased sailor from HMS *Barham* that would seal Helen's fate. While claiming to materialise his ghost, Helen told those attending a séance in Portsmouth that a torpedo from a German U-boat had sunk HMS *Barham*. The government had been desperately trying to conceal this information for fear of damaging public morale. Only several months after the event on 25 November 1941 did they reveal the loss of 841 lives. Helen was now considered a serious threat to national security, and plain clothes police attended her séances.

On the night of 19 January 1944, with plans for the D-Day landings on 6 June underway, the police raided a séance held by Helen. Officers tried to grab the ectoplasm from Helen's mouth, and although they failed Helen and three sitters were arrested. She was brought before magistrates and charged, at first under the 1824 Vagrancy Act, which would result in a maximum five shilling fine. Helen was denied bail and held in Holloway Prison, London for four days. By the time of her trial at the Old Bailey in March 1944, her charge had been amended to the more serious contravention of the 1735 Witchcraft Act through fraudulent spiritual activity, as well as several lesser charges.

Under the English Judicial System, the burden of proof is on the prosecution to establish guilt beyond a reasonable doubt, but the police had been unable to find any props to suggest that Helen's séance had been faked. Their evidence appeared extremely thin and instead of the onus being on the prosecution to prove their case the seven-day trial seemed to focus instead on proving whether or not Helen was in fact a genuine medium. Witness after witness was produced to testify to the authenticity of her gift. One such witness, James Herries, a Justice of the Peace, respected psychic investigator and chief reporter of the *Scotsman* swore that he had seen the famous author Sir Arthur Conan Doyle materialise at one of Helen's sittings. Despite such eminent witnesses for the defence, it took just half an hour for the jury to find Helen guilty of conspiracy to contravene the 1735 Witchcraft Act but not guilty on all other charges. She left the dock in tears, reportedly claiming "I never hee'd so mony lies in a' my life". A request for an appeal to the House of Lords was denied, though in a rare example of Scots and English Law Societies joining forces, these bar councils jointly claimed her case to be a travesty of justice.

Helen served her nine-month jail sentence in Holloway Prison, where warders refused to lock her cell door. During her confinement she was visited by warders, inmates and many others seeking spiritual guidance, among them the Prime Minister, Sir Winston Churchill. Churchill was a member of the Grand Ancient Order of Druids and a devout believer in psychic powers. On hearing of the Helen Duncan trial he tried to stop what he described as 'obsolete tomfoolery'. Churchill's civil servants were overruled by the paranoid security services, who were determined to incarcerate the medium while the Allies invaded Normandy. Had they been of a different mindset they might have tried to employ the talents they so obviously believed Helen possessed. It is thought that during his visits to Holloway, Churchill promised Helen that he would make amends and in 1951 the Witchcraft Act was at last repealed. Spiritualism was recognised as a religion by an Act of Parliament passed in 1954, although fraudulent mediums could still be prosecuted.

When Helen Duncan left prison on 22 September 1944, she swore that she would never hold another séance. It was a promise she could not keep and in November 1956 the police were again suspicious of her. During a raid on an address in Nottingham, constables grabbed hold of Helen, strip-searched her and took photographs of her whilst she was still in a trance. According to spiritualists, these were all actions that could cause the ectoplasm to leave the body too quickly, potentially causing fatal damage to the medium. However, Helen already had a long history of ill-health when she was rushed to hospital soon after the incident.

Despite Churchill's promise, the 1951 reforms had been of no benefit to the gifted Scottish housewife, who became the last person to be imprisoned under the 1735 Witchcraft Act. Five weeks after that final police raid she was dead.

Chapter Sixteen

'Queens Amang the Heather'

Jessie Murray from Buckie, a little old lady dressed in black stood up and sang a beautiful tune. It was 'Skippin' Barfit through the Heather':

As I was walkin' doon yon hill
It was a summer evenin',
It was there I spied a bonny lass
Skippin' barfit through the heather ...

Oh but she was neatly dressed,
She neither needed hat nor feather;
She was the queen amang them a',
Skippin' barfit through the heather.

The event Jessie was singing at, the First People's Festival Ceilidh, took place in the Oddfellows Hall in Edinburgh on 31 August 1951. Jessie was just one of the many singers of traditional Scottish ballads, including Jeannie Robertson, and Belle Stewart, who left behind a rich legacy of traditional songs and tunes, which, until the early fifties, had gone unrecorded.

For three hundred years Scotland's music was divided into two forms, the sacred and the secular. Sacred music was written down, but traditional folk ballads were handed down orally from generation to generation. Ballads were once a means of carrying news from one community to another and have become an invaluable source of information about Scottish society at the time when they were created. When the popularity of traditional Scottish music began to decline in the mid-nineteenth century, many of the great folk songs seemed to disappear from mainstream entertainment. However, the first Edinburgh People's Festival marked the beginning of a revival of Scottish Folk music that would continue throughout the 1960s and 70s.

The growing shift of opinion at the end of the Second World War made the period ripe for a revival of folk, or traditional, music. The 1945 election returned a Labour Government, with a large majority and this gave a huge amount of credibility to working people. Songs celebrating the lives of ordinary people now represented the hopes and fears of a generation. In 1948, on the twenty-fifth anniversary of his death, Glasgow celebrated the life of teacher and Communist John Maclean, imprisoned for his beliefs. 'The John Maclean March' was written by songwriter and collector Hamish Henderson for the event and it became the first new song of the revival.

The musical renaissance in Scotland was also realised in the establishment of the Edinburgh International Festival, the birth of Scottish Opera and the growing reputation of the Scottish National Orchestra. At the same time many felt the need for a centre for the study of Scottish traditional life. In 1949 an advisory board on postgraduate Scottish Studies was set up at Edinburgh University. In 1951 the department received its official name, the School of Scottish Studies, and began carrying out research into Gaelic and Scots music, social history and archaeology. Later it opened a folk-tale archive and a state-of-the-art laboratory to record songs for preservation.

Queen Elizabeth the First of Scotland

The Stone of Scone, the Scottish Coronation Stone, was reclaimed from Westminster Abbey on Christmas Day 1950 by four Scottish students and taken to Arbroath Abbey. Several poems and songs inspired by the repatriation appeared, seeming to confirm a re-emerging of Scottish national identity. Rumours spread that a replica of the stone had been made and this forgery was eventually returned to Westminster and used for Elizabeth II's coronation. After the coronation in 1953, protest songs sprang up; one, the 'Coronation Coronach', sung to the Orange tune 'The Sash' protested against the new Queen's title of Elizabeth II, when Scotland had never had an Elizabeth I. As one Scottish National Party member pointed out, 'Ye cannae have a second cup o' tea if ye have nae had a first.'

Between the recovery of the stone and Queen Elizabeth's coronation two events took place that would play a major part in the Scottish musical revival: the School of Scottish Studies was established, and the first Edinburgh People's Festival was held. Many Scots felt that the Edinburgh Festival started in 1947 had not offered a fair representation of traditional Scottish culture. Although some formal folk events had taken place at the festival, the informal and spontaneous ceilidhs were held in private houses. Many citizens welcomed both local and visiting folk musicians, actors, poets and artists all eager to participate in this 'new' musical experience.

The Edinburgh Labour Festival Committee was set up in 1951, with representatives from the Labour Party, the Co-operative Movement, the Edinburgh Trades Council, various trade unions including the Musician's Union, and some Scottish members of the Worker's Music Association. Among them was Janey Buchan, a member of the Communist Party until the Soviet invasion of Hungary in 1956 when she joined the Labour party and went on to become a Member of the European Parliament from 1979–94. For Janey, the First People's Festival was the beginning of a life-long involvement with performers, theatre groups and folksingers who mixed politics and entertainment.

These organised ceilidhs were set up to achieve two goals; to modify the elitist nature of the festival with its high ticket prices and to include working-class culture in the programme. The last of these festivals in ceilidh form was held in 1955, yet the music that had enthralled a variety of audiences continued to grow in popularity, becoming an integral part of the Edinburgh Fringe festival. It has also formed the basis of the folk clubs, which have appeared throughout Scotland. The first folk club was started by Morris Blythman, a languages teacher at Allan Glen's School in Glasgow. The club was held at the school after lessons and the pupils, who started out singing Glasgow street songs, such as 'My Maw's a Millionaire', were soon entertaining Women's Institutes and Co-operative organisations with traditional Scots songs.

Hamish Henderson, employed by the School of Scottish Studies at Edinburgh University, began visiting the folk concerts held at the school and evening ceilidhs at Maurice Blythman's home. These clubs and gatherings were then dominated by male organisers, singers and musicians. But soon the Blythmans were inviting guests to perform at the concerts, including a female singer and song-collector, Jeannie Robertson. Jeannie was an Aberdeenshire traveller, who could tell stories as well as sing ballads, lyric songs, bairn-sangs and the odd bawdy song such as 'Never wed an auld Man'. Hamish Henderson had tracked Jeannie down to her Aberdeen home in 1953 after learning of her at Blythman's concerts. Suspicious, she challenged the stranger on her doorstep to tell her the opening line of the hundred and sixty-third ballad published by Francis Child. Henderson answered correctly 'The Battle of Harlaw' and also obliged her by quoting the first words.

Jeannie's cousin, Belle Stewart was another traveller singled out by Henderson and the School of Scottish Studies. Belle was born on the banks of the River Tay at Caputh, near Blairgowrie, while her father was fishing for pearls. Just as Belle was born, he is said to have pulled a prize pearl from the Tay, which he later compared to his new daughter. However, the MacGregor family lived a precarious life, sleeping in bow tents, which they moved from site to site around the Highlands, often in a pram when they could not afford a horse and cart.

Belle's father died aged 32, after choking on his own vomit as he slept off a drinking session in the family cart, during the journey to Blairgowrie. In a biography of her mother, Belle's daughter, Sheila Stewart, describes how her grandmother sought help from the local doctor, taking the nine-month-old Belle in her arms. The doctor showed little concern, and took his time to examine Belle's father, who was then stretched out in the coach shed. Apparently the doctor later told a shopkeeper "Oh well, why worry? He was only a tinker".

Afraid that social workers would take her children away from her, Belle's mother stopped travelling and settled into a house in Perthshire. Unlike gypsies who originated in Egypt, the travellers, or tinkers, were indigenous to the British Isles and known for their metal-working skills. The Scots word *tinkler* means to solder or mend, suggesting the sound made by working with tin or metal. By the 1950s, settled communities saw travellers as social outcasts. Few appreciated the role of the traveller passing through the towns, bringing news, as well as mending, soldering and doing odd jobs. For farmers and landowners, the seasonal help offered by travellers played an important part in harvesting their crops. Gatherings such as the berry picking at Blairgowrie were an important social as well as economic part of the travellers' calendar, bringing families and friends together. The great family meetings and ceilidhs at the strawberry and raspberry picking were the inspiration for one of Belle Stewart's most well-known songs, 'The Berry Fields of Blair'.

Worse than the Devil Himsel'

The travellers' lifestyle was a rich but hard existence, especially for women, who made baskets, hawked goods, collected rags and did seasonal agricultural work as well as all the domestic tasks. As was also the case in non-travelling communities at the time, domestic violence was not uncommon and most of the womenfolk accepted a beating without complaint. Divorce among travellers, on the other hand, was rare.

According to her daughter, Belle heard an old ploughman sing a song 'When Micky comes home' while she was tattie-howking (digging potatoes) near Blairgowrie:

But when Micky comes home I get battered,
He batters me all black and blue,
And if I say a word I get scattered
From the kitchen right ben to the room.

So I'll go an I'll get blue bleezin' blind drunk,
Just to give Micky a warnin',
And just for spite I will stay out all night
And come rollin' home drunk in the mornin'.

Oh but whisky I ne'ver was a lover,
But what can a puir wumman do?
I'll go and I'll drown all me sorrows
But I wish I could drown Micky too.

In the song there is no reason for Micky to batter his wife. Ailie Munro in her book *Folk Music Revival in Scotland* (1996) quotes the singer Jean Redpath as having said this is the only Scots song she has heard of in which a woman is shown to be drinking '... and this fact certainly doesn't reflect the truth!'

Belle may have felt that the story would lack credibility if the wife was not held to blame for her own troubles and she added a first verse of her own. Her version tells us that in Mickey's mind his wife provoked the beatings by marrying him for his money:

Oh friends I have a sad story,
A very sad story tae tell:
I married a man for his money
But he's worse than the devil himsel'.

As well as collecting songs and stories from fellow travellers, Belle was able to immerse herself in the rich musical heritage of the family she married into. Alex Stewart, her second cousin, proposed to Belle after hearing her sing 'If I was a Blackbird' and the two married secretly in 1925. Their union would have been frowned upon within the traveller community, due to their close family connection. Alex's father, a champion piper, was the subject of the popular drinking song 'Jock Stewart, A Man You Don't Meet Every Day' recorded by The Dubliners and the Pogues. His grandfather, 'Big Jimmy' Stewart, allegedly died on his way home from busking, beaten to death by a group of Irishmen when he refused to play a tune they requested.

In the early 1950s, the younger members of the Stewart family made the first recordings of old Scottish ballads in London, after a visit to the family home by folk-singer Ewan MacColl. Hamish Henderson invited the whole family to perform at a concert in Edinburgh in 1954 and the Stewarts took the stage alongside 'Auld Galoot' (Davie Stewart), Jeannie Robertson, and Jimmy MacBeath. Later that year, Peter Kennedy and Douglas Kennedy visited them in Blairgowrie and made more recordings. Belle, Alex and their four children began performing in folk clubs, where they found people treated them with respect.

The Scottish folk revival ensured not only that the old songs and culture survived and that travelling folk were given the recognition they deserved, but it also renewed a sense of a Scottish identity, which had lain dormant for many years. A popular duo on the folk circuit were the Corries, Roy Williamson and Ronnie Browne. The pair met at Edinburgh College of Art in 1955 and formed a musical partnership that was to last more than 30 years. In the mid 1960s Roy wrote the immortal anthem that would have Scots everywhere thinking about their heritage and cause the Scottish Nationalist party membership to more than double in the last half of the decade.

But we can still rise now and be the nation again
That stood against him, proud Edward's army
And sent him homeward to think again

Chapter Seventeen

Flowers of Scotland

Lay the proud Usurpers low!
Tyrants fall in every foe!
Liberty's in every blow!
Let us do – or die!

(Robert Burns, 'Robert Bruce's
March to Bannockburn', 1793)

At five o'clock on Christmas morning 1950, Kay Matheson, a Glasgow University student from Inverasdale in the western Highlands, sat behind the wheel of a Ford Anglia parked in a lane by Westminster Abbey. As a tall figure moved through the door of Poets' Corner and into the light, Kay drove the car forward. The approaching figure, Ian Hamilton, told her to move the car back as their two accomplices still in the abbey were not yet ready to leave. Kay explained that a policeman had seen her and was making his way over the road. Hamilton pulled Kay into his arms and the pair pretended to be a courting couple. The police constable approached them and suggested they find somewhere else to park, but he seemed in no hurry to leave, removing his helmet and lighting a cigarette.

From behind a hoarding in the lane, Kay heard a scraping sound and muffled thuds. She engaged the policeman in conversation, raising her voice and laughing at his replies. Eventually, Kay asked the policeman to show her the way to a car park. She started the engine, jerked the clutch in and out and let the car veer from side to side, her driving designed to hold the constable's attention. When she reached the Old Palace Yard, Kay put her foot down. Back at Westminster Abbey, two other members of her group, Gavin Vernon and Alan Stuart had now freed the Stone of Scone from under the Coronation Chair.

The stone, a large block of red sandstone with chisel markings on the top, was linked to St Columba, who is said to have used it as a travelling altar. For centuries Scottish Kings sat upon the stone to be crowned. In the *Chronica Gentis Scottorum*, John of Fordun, a fourteenth century chronicler describes the elaborate ceremonies held at Scone, in Perthshire:

> *So the King [Alexander III] sat down upon the royal throne – that is the Stone – while the earls and other nobles, on bended knee strewed their garments under his feet, before the stone. Now this stone is reverently kept in that same monastery, for the consecration of the kings of Alba and no king was ever wont to reign in Scotland, unless he had first on receiving the name of King, sat upon this stone at Scone, which, by the kings of old, had been appointed the capital of Alba.*

In 1296, Edward I of England raided Scone Abbey and stole the Stone, taking it to Westminster. Despite the loss of the stone, and Edward having returned to attack the abbey two years later, Robert the Bruce was crowned King of Scotland there by Isabel of Fife on 25 March 1306. Some of Bruce's strongest and bravest supporters were women such as Isabel and Christiana, Lady of the Isles, who supplied him with galleys and troops.

Isabel of Fife was married to John Comyn, Earl of Buchan but it was her family line that gave Isobel the right to inaugurate the kings of Scotland. When Robert the Bruce killed a kinsman of the Earl of Buchan, known as the Red Comyn, Isabel's husband turned against Bruce. Isabel defied and abandoned Comyn; taking some of her husband's men and horses, she rode to Scone. There she performed the rite of enthronement and Bruce became king of Scotland.

Edward I was furious and when Isabel was captured at Tain along with Bruce's wife and family, he had her taken to Berwick Castle and locked in an iron cage. She would spend the next few years caged in the walls of the castle. Edward is reported to have ordered:

> *As she did not strike with the sword, she shall not perish by the sword ... let her be closely confined in an abode of stone and iron made in the shape of a cross, let her be hung up out of doors in the open air at Berwick, that both in life and after her death, she may be a spectacle and eternal reproach to travellers.*

Isabel survived her ordeal and in June 1310 she was placed in a Carmelite nunnery in Berwick, then released into the care of Henry Beaumont three years later.

The Caledonian Job

When the Stone of Scone was freed from Westminster Abbey by four Scottish Nationalist students on 25 December 1950 it was first of all hidden in a field in Kent. Meanwhile police the length and breadth of Scotland looked for a couple with Scottish accents, travelling in a Ford Anglia. When the gang went to retrieve the stone from its hiding place, a sympathetic mason had to be found to repair the stone as it had split down an old crack when removed from under the Coronation Chair.

Nearly four months after its retrieval from Westminster Abbey, three men drove up to Arbroath Abbey, the site of the 1320 Declaration of Arbroath and carried the stone, draped in a saltire, along the main aisle before laying it at the high altar above the grave of King William the Lion of Scotland. Two unsigned letters were left on top of the stone, one addressed to the General Assembly of The Church of Scotland as 'Successors to the Abbots of Scone' and another to King George VI, which contained the words:

> *That in their actions they, as loyal subjects have intended no indignity or injury to his Majesty or to the Royal Family. That they have been inspired in all that they have done by their deep love of his Majesty's realm of Scotland and by their desire to compel the attention of His Majesty's minister to the widely expressed demand of the Scottish people for a measure of self-government.*

Kay Matheson was questioned in relation to the repatriation of the stone but, like the three men involved she was never charged with an offence, and she began a career as a teacher. The Home Secretary stated that it was not in the public interest to prosecute the students. In truth, the people of Scotland had made it perfectly clear that there would be riots if charges were brought against the four. Although in 1950 unionism was at its most popular, there was still a lot of feeling for the stone as it traditionally belonged to the people of Scotland, not their rulers.

Before questioning Kay Matheson, the police's major female suspect for the heist was Wendy Wood. An artist, writer, and radical nationalist, Wendy had been involved in a previous failed attempt to liberate the stone.

Wendy Wood: *The Cause*

Wendy Wood believed in a free and independent Scotland but she made no secret of her cause and had no intention of committing it to the vindication of posterity. She became a one-woman protest movement for an independent Scotland and campaigned using legal and illegal tactics, which occasionally led to her imprisonment. She was arrested in a protest march against the British Union of Fascists in 1937 and imprisoned for 60 days in Duke Street Prison, Glasgow, for refusing to pay National Insurance. Later, a term in Holloway Prison for holding a rally in London, against the removal of the National Insurance Board from Glasgow to Newcastle, led to her campaign for prison reform.

Born Gwendoline Emily Meacham, in Kent, Wendy was the grand-daughter of Eilidh Ross, a Scottish Highland crofter's daughter. Wendy took her mother's surname, Wood in 1927. When challenged as to her Scottish birthright, Wendy would retaliate by pointing out, 'One does not have to be a horse to be born in a stable'. Wendy's mother told the Meacham children Scottish folk tales, including the adventures of William Wallace and every Sunday afternoon, her father, a research chemist, showed the children slides of Scotland. Much of Wendy's time was taken up with painting and drawing and the figures she painted into her landscapes indicated her interest in folk and fairy legends. In her work there was a clear relationship between nature and her romantic visions of Scottish national identity.

By the age of 17, Wendy had benefited from a liberal education and attended evening classes at the Westminster School of Art under Walter Sickert. After she left with a Certificate of the Royal Drawing School, Wendy continued to develop the visual imagination she would put to good use in her political career. At public meetings, she used flags, badges, banners and road signs to good effect.

After working for a while as a nursery nurse, Wendy married Walter Cuthbert, a shoe manufacturer, in 1913 and the newly-weds settled in Ayr, where Walter's business was situated. When his investments crashed, the pair moved to Dundee, where Wendy, then known as Gwen Cuthbert, became a storyteller for the BBC's *Children's Hour* programme. The couple had two daughters but the marriage did not last, and Gwen left her husband, her home, and her job to move to Edinburgh, where she renamed herself 'Wendy Wood'.

Impressed by Keir Hardie, the Independent Labour Party's founder's policy on Home Rule, Wendy had joined the Scottish League and the Home Rule Association. When she met Lewis Spence, a linguist, mythologist and folklorist, it was not difficult for him to persuade her to join the Scottish National Movement. She became a co-founder of the National Party of Scotland in 1928 and supported Spence's campaign as Nationalist Candidate for North Midlothian, a seat he won.

Many of Wendy's political escapades would today be referred to as performance art: subversive, anti–authoritarian, humorous and irreverent. After the Bannockburn rally of 1932 – a spectacular event headed by the one of the Scottish Nationalist co-founders, Cunninghame-Graham riding on a white charger – she led a group of nationalists into Stirling Castle, then an army barracks and tore down the union flag, replacing it with Scotland's lion rampant.

On 20 April 1934, the National Party of Scotland merged with the smaller Scottish Party, becoming the Scottish National Party (SNP). Founding members included the poets Lewis Spence and Hugh MacDiarmid, novelist Compton MacKenzie and author Florence Marian McNeill, who became Vice President. The young Scottish National Party had two main problems. The National Party of Scotland had been made up mostly of fundamentalists eager to concentrate on independence, while Scottish Party members were more moderate, gradualists who wanted to achieve independence through policies such as devolution. Often referred to as the 'intellectual party', these differences, as well as policies for an independent Scotland, would be debated for many years to come.

In its early days, the party encountered a lack of success in fighting elections, perhaps due to lack or organisation and funding. In the 1935 General Election, the SNP contested eight seats and won none. Its first success did not come until a decade later, when Robert MacIntyre won the Wishaw by-election for the SNP, only to lose the seat in the general election months later. Wendy Wood also stood in the same election, contesting the Bridgeton seat, but she too was unsuccessful.

During the late 1930s and early 40s, Wendy continued her protests. In 1937 she protested against the Blackshirts in Edinburgh and continued her fight to improve conditions in Scottish women's prisons. More civil disobedience followed in 1950, when she hung an effigy of the Secretary of State for Scotland in Glasgow and unrolled a Home Rule banner at the Highland games.

By now Wendy's relationship with Oulith MacAndreis (Oliver MacAndrew), the editor of *Smeddum* and *The Lion Rampant*, was coming to an end. The couple had set up home in a croft at Alt Ruig, next to Glenuig around 1939, but when MacAndreis admitted to being both married and a member of the IRA, Wendy left him. Although a believer in taking direct action, Wendy could never condone violence. She would though, continue her fight for Home Rule, addressing the General Assembly in May 1960, the first woman to do so since Lady Aberdeen in 1931. As part of her life-long campaign she went on hunger strike in 1972, when she was 80 years old. Wendy died in 1981 without seeing the realisation of her dream when 18 years later a devolved parliament returned to Holyrood.

Winnie Ewing & Margo MacDonald:

While the SNP were continuing their fight for independence, from 1956 onwards broadcasts on the pirate station Radio Free Scotland saw an increase in party membership. As the BBC sound channel closed down at 11pm with 'God Save the Queen', Radio Free Scotland would come on air with the words "Radio Free Scotland Calling", broadcasting from the top of several different houses for around 20 minutes. Early broadcasts were comprised of a mixture of propaganda and Scottish folk songs, as the new passion for folk clubs had brought music into the Nationalist movement.

At this time Scotland was beginning to see a change of attitude towards national identity. At the beginning of the 1960s there were some 20 branches of the SNP with around 2,000 members and by the end of the decade, several hundred branches and around 65,000 members. Part of the reason for the surge in Nationalist sentiment was greater criticism of Westminster's control of Scottish affairs and the change in BBC policy in the mid-sixties. On 29 September 1965 the SNP were given their first five-minute television Party Political Broadcast on the BBC. It was delivered by the then SNP leader, William Wolfe, and watched by 1,250,000 people.

The time was ripe for the SNP to fight and win an election in Scotland and when a by-election was held in Hamilton in 1967, the SNP candidate chosen was a 38-year-old solicitor, Winifred Margaret Ewing. Winnie Ewing won with 18,395 votes and the party at SNP headquarters continued all night. When it was time for the new Hamilton MP to take up her seat at Westminster, thousands turned up to wave her off, some playing pipes and singing on the platform. As the train pulled out of the station, a massive ceilidh began on the train and many more were held throughout Scotland.

Until the 1967 by-election the Labour party had not seen the SNP as serious opposition. Labour MPs turned hostile, as they realised that if Hamilton could fall to the SNP so could their other strongholds. Scholar, orator and patriot, Oliver Brown has famously been quoted as saying that the result 'caused a shiver to run along the Scottish Labour benches looking for a spine to run up'.

The spine they chose to exercise on belonged to Winnie Ewing. In an interview with BBC Radio Scotland, Winnie commented that at Westminster in an age of chivalry, the Welsh, the Irish and the English were always kind and so were the Tories, but the Labour MPs were vicious. She says she was stalked by Labour MPs through the dark corridors of Westminster after the lights were turned off and felt so intimidated she lost two stone in weight. When some old friends in the Labour party heard of her predicament, Winnie was taken to the office of Prime Minister Harold Wilson and persuaded to tell her story. The intimidation ceased. The SNP lost Hamilton in the next general election, but Winnie Ewing went on to win the Highlands and Island seat in 1979 and was elected to the first European Parliament where she became known as 'Madame Ecosse'.

As Winnie Ewing was celebrating her success, Margo MacDonald, another female supporter of the Scottish Nationalist Party, was managing the Hoolets Nest Pub in High Blantyre, with her first husband and two daughters. It would be another six years before she took her seat on the tartan express. As she left for the House of Commons Margo said that she would rather be sitting in a Scottish parliament and that she did, but not for another 26 years.

Margo MacDonald was born in Hamilton in 1943, and attended Dunfermline College of Physical Education. An outspoken left-wing candidate, Margo contested and won one of Labour's heartland seats for the SNP at the Govan by-election of 1973. Despite her party's anti-nuclear policy, she supported the development of the nuclear power stations in Ayrshire. In her maiden speech, Margo referred to her constituency as a community reduced to only two working shipyards and stated, 'If we are to have a future for the Scottish steel industry and security for the people who are employed in that industry and related industries an iron-ore terminal is a necessity".

Unlike Winnie Ewing, Margo seems to have been well received by her fellow Scots MPs. After her maiden speech, the Hon Thomas Galbraith, MP for Glasgow, Hillhead, rose to his feet: "I begin by congratulating the honourable member for Glasgow, Govan (Mrs MacDonald) on a well prepared and attractively delivered speech. If all that I heard did not please my ears, everything that my eye saw was a delight". The member for Greenock, Dr Dickson Mabon added, "The honourable gentleman said that it was necessary in almost all circumstances to have beauty and the beast. Certainly, she is the beauty".

It would seem that although Scottish women had fought their way to Westminster, the battle against overt sexism was still to be won.

Chapter Eighteen

A Woman's Right To Choose

Advances in education, gaining the vote, improvements in working conditions and changes in the divorce laws would all play their part over the years in enhancing Scottish women's lives. However, the twentieth century would see the removal of the burden which had ruled women's lives: unwanted pregnancies and the dangers of childbirth. Discoveries in midwifery, the introduction of the oral contraception pill and the 1967 Abortion Act, would finally ensure that women's bodies were no longer public property.

Since the nineteenth century, women had enjoyed access to pain relief during childbirth. In the nineteenth century doctors, like Sir James Young Simpson, Chair of Medicine and Midwifery at Edinburgh University, had explored forms of anaesthesia. Keen to alleviate the labour pains of his patients, Simpson became interested in the possibilities of anaesthesia in surgery and childbirth. Rejecting laughing gas and ether, he began to experiment with various chemicals until he discovered chloroform. The first women to be anaesthetised during labour were so grateful for the relief that one woman apparently christened her daughter 'Anaesthesia'. Chloroform did not become widely available straight away, for there was much opposition to the new drug from the Church, on the grounds that pain in childbirth was divinely ordained.

Although significant advances in the method of delivery had already been made, many women were still dying in childbirth as a result of infection. Doctors were unaware of the necessity for cleanliness, and the fact that diseases such as puerperal fever were spread by bacteria. The discovery by Dr Joseph Lister, in the mid-1800s of the importance of sterile conditions and the use of carbolic acid saw hospital mortality rates drop.

This new knowledge, however, had little effect on the practice of birth control. With fewer mothers and babies perishing in childbirth, the population was rising rapidly. Doctors warned that infanticide and abortion were now once again on the increase, as parents could not afford to support such large families. By the 1890s even some within the Church, once bitterly opposed to limiting the size of families, were beginning to change their minds.

Early condoms were made of sheep intestines, but not widely used, as they were expensive and fairly difficult to obtain. During the nineteenth century condoms began to be produced from vulcanized rubber, a strong elastic material, which men were instructed to wash out and reuse. Latex manufacturing processes improved in the 1930s and soon it was possible to produce a thin, pliant and inexpensive product, which was widely used in the Second World War.

During the First World War around ten per cent of all servicemen were thought to have suffered from venereal disease, and on the outbreak of the Second World War, the British Army was determined to raise awareness among servicemen of the dangers of poor sexual hygiene. According to the advice issued by the army, women were the source of VD, yet no advice was relayed to the women the soldiers may have been infecting. For those who contracted a disease, during the 1940s treatment was becoming more widely available, and medicines more effective. By 1944 an average case of gonorrhoea could be treated in five days while the patient remained on duty, and syphilis could be treated with a series of injections of Bismuth and Arspenamine.

Syphilis first appears as a sore or chancre, then as a rash sometimes accompanied by mild fever. If untreated, the disease then passes into its latent phase, which can last from ten to twenty years. Many Second World War servicemen returned home with untreated syphilis. Psychiatric hospitals in the 1950s and 1960s contained many patients in the tertiary stages of the disease. In its final stage, the disease attacks vital organs and sometimes the nervous system, in some cases causing blindness, deafness, and a condition known as general paresis of the insane.

Some men carrying syphilis either did not know that they had the disease or were too embarrassed to go to their doctor with what was considered a socially unacceptable disease. As a result, they often transmitted the disease to their unsuspecting wives and, as the chancre and rash are often much harder to detect in the female organs, many women lived unaware of the time bomb they carried. A syphilitic mother was also at risk of passing the disease onto her unborn child during the foetal development and nearly half of all children infected with syphilis die shortly before or after birth. It is said by some that the disease attacks the innocent as well as the sinner, as the disease causes the same amount of degeneration in an infant as in an adult.

Marie Stopes: *family planning pioneer*

Families were growing smaller, developing into more economically manageable units, as the twentieth century progressed. This was in part due to the 'family planning' clinics founded by Marie Stopes, an Edinburgh botanist. Marie was educated at St George's School For Girls in Edinburgh and graduated from University College London with a BSc in botany and geology in 1902. Two years later she was awarded a PhD in Munich for her work on fossilised plants.

Marie's scientific career flourished, and whilst in Canada she met Reginald Ruggles Gates, a fellow botanist, whom she married in March 1911. Their union was not a happy one and in 1914 Marie had the marriage annulled on the grounds of non-consummation. She claimed that due to her ignorance of sex, it had taken her two years to realise that her husband was impotent and she was still a virgin. This unhappy period of her life inspired Marie to write *Married Love*, a guide to sex and equality in marital relationships, which was published in 1918. It was a great success, although controversial, and later that year she published a sequel, *Wise Parenthood*, which dealt explicitly with birth control.

With financial support from her second husband, Henry Roe, as well as Margaret Sanger, the American birth control pioneer,

Marie opened a family planning clinic in London in 1921. Through her writings and public speaking in favour of family planning she became a controversial figure. Her fame brought her into opposition with both the medical profession and the Catholic Church. In 1923 she was involved in a much publicised libel case, but nonetheless was able to break many taboos by introducing public discussion of these issues. Her clinics spread throughout Britain and still survive today.

Stopes's friend and colleague, the activist Margaret Sanger had been the first to open a family planning clinic in America. In 1951 she met Gregory Pincus, the scientist who created a test tube rabbit, at a dinner party in New York. She was able to persuade Pincus to work on a birth control pill for women. EnAvid, the first pill to inhibit ovulation, was prescribed in the UK as a contraceptive from 1961, at first only to married women. In Scotland with its tradition of Calvinist teaching, sex before marriage was heavily frowned upon and this attitude persisted.

The oral contraceptive was an important step forward for many married women, as it allowed them to plan their families and limit the number of children they had. For society in general, it curbed the number of big families that were the norm during the pre-war years.

Other social changes took longer to evolve. In the late 1960s the debate over abortion would cause far more debate and controversy than the pill had instigated earlier in the decade. In response to evidence of unsafe illegal abortion and resulting maternal mortality, the Scottish Liberal MP David Steel brought a private member's bill into parliament. This would later become the Abortion Act 1967, which is still the law governing abortions in Scotland, England and Wales. Technically the law did not legalise abortions, but rather it provided a legal defence for those authorising them and performing the surgery.

Those pushing for the decriminalisation of abortion painted a tragic picture of the women they wished to help, among them alcoholics, mothers incapable of coping with another child, and those whose husbands were violent drunkards, in prison or simply absent. These women were part of the same group who had struggled on unaided throughout most of history. Opponents took a similar view to the authorities who had introduced the Concealment of Pregnancy Act in 1690, describing women who wished to terminate a pregnancy as selfish, irrational and irresponsible. In this polarised debate neither group appeared to consider single women who either could not cope with bringing up a child alone, or would consider a termination for health reasons. Possibly the pro-choice lobby believed that employing this argument would appear to promote promiscuity.

However, the arguments of both camps presented women as inadequate, incapable of making their own decisions. When the resulting Abortion Act came into effect in 1967, doctors had more say in the procedure than in any other form of surgery. An abortion needed to be agreed by two doctors and could only be performed under certain conditions, one being that to continue with the pregnancy involved a great risk to the woman's physical health. Other conditions considered include danger to the prospective mother's mental health, the well-being of her existing children and her actual or foreseeable future. Some would say all factors of which the women concerned would have the best knowledge and therefore be the best judge.

The abortion act brought cries of 'a woman's right to choose' from the growing feminist movement and was instrumental in the fight for the equal rights that followed. Women had obtained greater, although imperfect, autonomy over their bodies and minds with the invention of the oral contraception pill and the introduction of the Abortion Act. Since the Concealment of Pregnancy Act of 1690, women have fought a three hundred year-long battle for equality. One more right has still to be acknowledged by writers and historians, and that is a woman's right to have the events of her life recorded, so that generations to come may learn of the important contribution women make to any society.

Select Bibliography

Anderson, J., *The Ladies of the Covenant* (Blackie and Son, 1891)

Arnot, H., *History of Edinburgh, from the earliest accounts to the year 1780* ... (Thomas Turnbull, 1816)

Blair, A., *Scottish Tales* (Richard Drew Publishing, 1987)

Brown, P., *Whores, Harlots & Wanton Women: the Story of Illicit Sex* (Amberley, 2008)

Brown, Y. G., Craig, M., Ferguson R., eds, *Twisted Sisters: Women, Crime and Deviance in Scotland Since 1400* (Tuckwell Press, 2002)

Carswell C., *The Life of Robert Burns* (Chatto and Windus, 1930)

Craig, C., *The Tears That Made the Clyde* (Argyll Publishing, 2010)

Craig, M., *Damn Rebel Bitches: the Women of the '45* (Mainstream Publishing, 1997)

Docherty, M., *A Miner's Lass* (Lancashire Community Press, 1992)

Edwards, E.M., ed, *Scotland's Land Girls: Breeches, Bombers and Back Aches* (NMSE, 2010)

Ewan, E., Innes, S., Reynolds, S., eds, *The Biographical Dictionary of Scottish Women* (Edinburgh University Press, 2006)

Findlay, B., ed, *A History of Scottish Theatre* (Polygon, 1998)

Fry, M., *The Union: England, Scotland and the Treaty of 1707* (Birlinn, 2006)

Grant, E., *Memoirs of a Highland Lady* (John Murray, 1898)

Howrie, J., M'Gavin, W., *The Scots Worthies, Volume Second, Containing Their Last Words and Dying Testimonies* (W.R. MacPhun, 1830)

Joyce, F. 'Prostitution and the Nineteenth Century: In Search of the 'Great Social Evil'', *Reinvention: an International Journal of Undergraduate Research*, vol 1, issue 1 (University of Warwick, 2013)

King, E., *The Hidden History of Glasgow's Women* (Mainstream Publishing, 1993)

Leneman, L., & Mitchison, R., *Sin in the City: Sexuality and Social Control in Urban Scotland 1660–1780* (Scottish Cultural Press, 1998)

Milne, H.M., *Boswell's Edinburgh Journals 1767–1786* (Mercat Press, 2001)

Moreton, S., *Bonanzas and Jacobites: the Story of the Silver Glen* (NMSE Publishing Ltd, 2007)

Munro, A., *Folk Music Revival in Scotland: the Democratic Muse* (Scottish Cultural Press, 1996)

Pinkola Estes, C., *Women Who Run With Wolves* (Rider, 1992)

Pugh, R.J.M. *The Deil's Ain* (Harlaw Heritage, 2001)

Robertson, A. *http://crivensjingsandhelpmaboab.blogspot.co.uk/2013/04/16th-april-1745-culloden-moor-and.html*

Smout, T.C., *A History of the Scottish People 1560–1830* (Collins Clear Type Press, 1969)

Symonds, D.A., *Weep not for Me: Women, Ballads and Infanticide in Early Modern Scotland* (Pennsylvania State University Press, 1997)

Whittington-Egan, M., *The Stockbridge Baby Farmer and Other Scottish Murder Stories* (Neil Wilson Publishing, 2001)

Williams, D., *The Horsieman, Memories of a Traveller 1928–58* (Birlinn Ltd, 1994)

Index